DI
A Political

MONOBINA GUPTA studied in Calcutta University and Jawaharlal Nehru University. She has worked as a journalist with the *Patriot*, the *Telegraph*, *Mail Today* and Indo-Asian News Service. Her first book, *Left Politics in Bengal: Time Travels among Bhadralok Marxists*, was published in 2010. This is her second book. She is currently working with the *Times of India*.

DIDI
A Political Biography

MONOBINA GUPTA

HarperCollins *Publishers* India
a joint venture with

New Delhi

First published in India in 2012 by
HarperCollins *Publishers* India
a joint venture with
The India Today Group

Copyright © Monobina Gupta 2012

ISBN: 978-93-5029-168-9

2 4 6 8 10 9 7 5 3 1

Monobina Gupta asserts the moral right to be identified as the author of this work.

The views and opinions expressed in this book are the author's own and the facts are as reported by her, and the publishers are not in any way liable for the same.

All rights reserved. No part of this publication may be reproduced, stored in a retrieval system, or transmitted, in any form or by any means, electronic, mechanical, photocopying, recording or otherwise, without the prior permission of the publishers.

HarperCollins *Publishers*
A-53, Sector 57, Noida, Uttar Pradesh 201301, India
77-85 Fulham Palace Road, London W6 8JB, United Kingdom
Hazelton Lanes, 55 Avenue Road, Suite 2900, Toronto, Ontario M5R 3L2
and 1995 Markham Road, Scarborough, Ontario M1B 5M8, Canada
25 Ryde Road, Pymble, Sydney, NSW 2073, Australia
31 View Road, Glenfield, Auckland 10, New Zealand
10 East 53rd Street, New York NY 10022, USA

Typeset in Minion 11/14
Jojy Philip, New Delhi 110 015

Printed and bound at
Nutech Print Services, Faridabad, India

For my parents
Milan Chandra and Manjari Gupta

Contents

Preface ix
1. Meet Mamata Banerjee 1
2. From Jadavpur to Delhi 23
3. The Making of Mamata Banerjee 61
4. The Singur–Nandigram–Lalgarh Journey 89
5. Taking Over the Cultural Space 113
6. The Performance of Politics 139
7. Preparing for the Transition 144
8. A Chief Minister in Waiting 175

Epilogue 189
Notes and References 201
Index 207
Acknowledgements 217

Preface

Mamata Banerjee has been known to evoke strong emotions. Her fans worship her fearlessness, her simple, ascetic lifestyle, even her melodramatic performances. To her political adversaries she is a stubborn fighter who has repeatedly returned to haunt them despite their attempts to browbeat her out of the political arena. Mamata reigns imperious and unchallenged over her somewhat amorphous party, the Trinamool Congress, which is now in power in West Bengal. In private conversations, Didi's party colleagues tell you how terrified they are of Mamata's tempestuousness and her mercurial temperament. But even among sceptics who look down upon her non-gentrified ways, the Trinamool Congress leader inspires grudging awe.

This book tries to capture some of the complexities that make Mamata Banerjee what she is. In order to comprehend the different aspects of her persona, which often contradict each other, I have tried to contextualize Mamata within a broader framework of Bengal's bhadralok culture and the religious and cultural elements which influence her politics and life. I have tried to understand Mamata's own perception of herself as a woman; her responses, if any, to feminism; the contradictions between her dictatorial and democratic impulses; and her appropriation of the Left's culture and radical politics in recent years.

Through a study of books authored by Mamata, and interviews with her colleagues and cultural and human rights activists, I have situated the subject in the larger context of thirty-four years of Left Front rule. Though she experimented with coalitions led both by the Congress and the BJP at the Centre and headed important ministries in the Central government, her attention was always focused on one goal: defeating the Left Front government and coming to power in Bengal.

Written during the run-up to West Bengal's historic 2011 polls, the book ends with Mamata's ascendancy to chief ministership. She has inherited a financially bankrupt and stagnating state, politicized to the core. Ironically, her predicament is somewhat like that of the Left Front when, through a bloody struggle against the Congress, it had first come to power in 1977. Hardened in the school of radical protests and agitations, the Marxists then knew little about governance and administration. Mamata, too, has followed a similar path. The people of Bengal now have high expectations from her and the new regime, not just for governance, but also for inaugurating a different political culture.

As the book goes into press, Mamata Banerjee has completed six months as chief minister. Many have done some hurried stock taking of her performance during this brief and dramatically eventful period. Some have pronounced harsh judgment, reprimanding her for continuing to be unpredictable and combative, and still acting more like a recalcitrant Opposition leader than the chief minister of a state. Less inclined to penning an early epitaph, more circumspect critics have adopted a calibrated approach in their assessment. Six months is too soon to come to any decisive conclusion—either by unequivocally endorsing, or by rubbishing her altogether. Nasty controversies have already erupted, dragging Mamata into the conflict zone of ideas, policies, politics and personalities. But this was hardly unforeseen.

In the latter part of the book I have attempted to underline the enormous challenges that lie ahead of the new ruling party and its supreme leader, as West Bengal entered a new political era in May 2010. As is usual with any regime change, the teething period in this case too has been prickly and problematic. In fact, in the case of West Bengal, political and governance shifts were decidedly more challenging, more fractious and riddled with both unexpected and expected pitfalls. Mamata has inherited a moribund political and administrative state. The first six months were bound to be critical. The new chief minister was expected to send the right signal not only to her electorate at home, but also to policymakers and the Congress-led UPA government in Delhi.

Two main charges levelled against the Trinamool chief have hinged on the subjects of economic reforms and Maoist insurgency. The recent high-pitched debate triggered by the Centre's decision to introduce 51 per cent FDI in multi-brand retail has dramatically brought out into the open the inherent tensions between the ruling Congress and Mamata Banerjee. Mamata's refusal to endorse the opening up of retail has finally forced the government to put the controversial policy on hold. Standing firmly by her party's stated position, Mamata argued that FDI in retail was going to hurt small traders and farmers. Already marked as 'anti-reform' and 'anti-industry', her hard line against FDI in retail has put her in the direct line of fire of large sections of the political and business classes, as well as the media. At the same time, though the Left will be loath to admit it, Mamata has managed—by stalling FDI—to play the role it aspires for. She has not shown any indications of turning her back on her party's commitment on issues of economic policy. Her stance has surely evoked disappointment among CPI-M leaders who want her to renege on commitments and desert the constituency that she had weaned away from them. Mamata, however, is not yet ready to give up the 'Leftist' profile she acquired with Singur and Nandigram. In that sense, her stance vis-à-vis FDI in retail should not come as a surprise to the Congress, which had courted an alliance with the Trinamool leader knowing fully well her stand on contentious issues like this. Paradoxically, with nineteen MPs and as the single largest UPA ally, Mamata has now stepped into the shoes of her Left adversaries.

The other serious allegation against the Trinamool chief, now whipped up with renewed vigour, revolves around her uneasy relationship with the Maoists. Towards the end of November 2011, rising tensions between Mamata and the Maoists led to a major showdown. Following killings of Trinamool workers, Mamata first served an ultimatum to the Maoists, asking them to lay down their arms. Not surprisingly, they refused and demanded that security forces be withdrawn from Jangalmahal. Mamata, however, went ahead and sanctioned a resumption of the security forces' operations, even as her critics came down heavily on her and accused her of political expediency. Once perceived as a Maoist ally in her battle against the Left, Mamata was blamed for doing an opportunistic about-turn. Shedding kid gloves, she now seemed ready to deal with the Maoists with an iron hand.

But the debate here is multilayered and complex, going beyond naïve and simplistic explanations. During the tribal upsurge in Lalgarh, the CPI-M had launched an acidic campaign, accusing Mamata of aiding and abetting Maoist violence in Jangalmahal. Undoubtedly, her political rhetoric at that time was ambivalent. She did indeed play down the issue in the interest of her ultimate goal of defeating the Left Front government. But to describe Mamata as being hand-in-glove with the insurrectionists would be a gross exaggeration. Her polemical claims aimed at the CPI-M—that there were no Maoists in Bengal—on the eve of assembly elections should not be taken at face value. It was part of the rhetoric of political performance at the time.

Let's not forget that Mamata—despite her recent alliances with Left-leaning intellectuals, artistes and activists—has always been essentially a political centrist at heart. The recent escalation in tension between her and the Maoists needs to be grounded in a context where after assuming power Mamata had given them enough leeway to abandon arms and come to the negotiating table for talks. She had kept the Central and state joint security forces operation in abeyance, which was one of her key manifesto commitments. But the negotiations did not work. Even as the chief minister announced a slew of development packages for Jangalmahal, the Maoists stepped up their offensive. With Mamata sanctioning resumption of security operations against the Maoists, the bonds between her and a sizeable section of Left-leaning intellectuals and human rights activists seem to be on the verge of snapping. The growing distance was manifest when the government-appointed interlocutors, mandated to negotiate with the Maoists, quit following the killing of prominent Maoist leader Koteshwar Rao, popularly known as Kishenji.

In the months ahead, the Maoist challenge is only likely to sharpen and deepen the conflict between a section of radical, Left-leaning people and Mamata. Her historic tensions with the Congress, starting with her bitter fight as a student and then youth activist with the West Bengal unit, are also likely to be a problem. A section of the Congress state unit has already taken to the streets, protesting some of the actions of the new regime. But the situation as it stands today is that the state Congress unit, weak as it is, needs Mamata for its survival more than she needs it. At the same time, given West Bengal's depleted financial resources, Mamata is dependent on the ruling Congress at the Centre. She is trying to negotiate a Bengal package to put the economy in some kind of an order. The UPA government has finally, at the end of a tussle, agreed to disburse Rs 8,750 crore. But Mamata is demanding Rs 10,000 crore.

There seems to be a perception, though mostly outside West Bengal and primarily in Delhi's corridors of power, that Mamata's charm is on the wane; that her voters are beginning to grow impatient with the slow pace of 'paribartan'. Recent incidents like the chief minister storming into a local police station and rescuing two of her party workers, earlier arrested for rioting, seemed to feed that negative impression. Critics who expect Mamata to fit the image of a bhadralok chief minister are disappointed that she is still sticking to her 'street-fighting' tactics. But the ground situation in West Bengal may not reflect this cynical assessment. For instance, in a parliamentary by-election held in Kolkata South on 30 November, state Trinamool Congress President Subrata Bakshi won by a record margin of 2,30,099 votes. No doubt the Trinamool Congress candidate had an advantage. Kolkata South, after all, had been Mamata's own constituency, from where she had won successive elections since 1991. But even with this inherent advantage, Bakshi's margin of victory was impressive.

Mamata's harshest critics accuse her of starting on the wrong foot by refusing to transform herself into the image of a 'bhadralok' politician. But, as I underline throughout this book, Mamata's 'otherness'—in terms of class, culture, language and gender—is indicative of larger changes that are afoot in Bengal's political culture. The complexities of this transformative process are bound to play themselves out in unexpected ways. Issues of governance—ranging from economic transformation to health, education, and most importantly the culture of political violence and patronage—will continue to dominate. In the long run, how Mamata addresses these challenges will determine her legacy as chief minister of Bengal.

1

Meet Mamata Banerjee

The year was 1983. Twenty-eight-year-old Mamata Banerjee was getting into the rhythm of active politics. And the All India Congress Committee (AICC)[1] was in full session in Kolkata. Three years ago, Indira Gandhi had returned to power from her political banishment; her son Rajiv Gandhi had been appointed AICC general secretary and septuagenarian Kamlapati Tripathi its working secretary.

Mamata was a volunteer in senior Congress leader Subrata Mukherjee's team. Her responsibility was to look after party VIPs, a tricky job that the irreverent young woman handled in her own unique way.

For instance, few twenty-somethings with serious political ambitions would dare to play a prank on Congress patriarch Tripathi, and that too one that subverts notions of caste purity. But then Mamata, even as a young girl, had quite an appetite for tomfoolery. Consider this story she tells in her autobiography *Struggle for Existence*. Mamata complains that, while Rajiv Gandhi did not have volunteers running errands for him, 'the problem was with the aged leader Kamlapati Tripathi'.[2] A high-caste Brahmin and a stickler for 'ritual purity', Kamlapati would only eat meals cooked by fellow Brahmins. 'Subrata-da told me, "He will eat food which has been cooked by a lady of the Brahmin caste only. For the morning, keep some juice of pistachios, cashew nuts and raisins."'[3] Mamata passed on these instructions to her colleague Anima Chatterjee, who had the 'right credentials'. Anima, who was struggling with a busy schedule, said she would need two helpers. Mamata writes, 'I replied, "Wait, we will outwit the old gentleman. Two of my non-Brahmin colleagues will do the cooking and, Anima, you can serve the food."'[4] So they did. 'Everything went according to plan. Perhaps what we had done was wrong! Tripathiji is no more. If he was alive he would have fired me.'[5]

Mamata has brought this playful streak with her all the way from her days as a Congress party volunteer till now when she is the most powerful politician in West Bengal. As recently as December 2010, she playfully dunked an unsuspecting Sovan Chatterjee, mayor of Kolkata and a Trinamool Congress leader, in a children's swimming pool on a cold winter day. It goes without saying that the man couldn't have been pleased, but could do little more than put a pleasant face in spite of his dripping wet clothes, the chill, and the flush of embarrassment he must have felt. Trinamool workers do not normally challenge Mamata's authority.

These pranks—separated as they are by time and context—throw light on the contradictory, paradoxical figure that is Mamata Banerjee. There isn't one analytic lens you can look through to make sense of her. She can be conventional, even traditional, and still subvert caste norms. She can casually dupe a senior leader who she thinks is being irrational. She can terrorize fellow party members, and still enchant and mesmerize them. She doesn't fit the frame of mainstream politicians or conform to the stereotypes about prominent public figures. It isn't easy then to tackle the combustive, nomenclature-defying subject that is Mamata Banerjee.

So we must eschew linear projections and unidimensional definitions if we are to understand her. The personality of the Trinamool Congress leader is fragmented, somewhat dishevelled. The personal and the political are enmeshed, often even in collision with each other. Mamata's flagrant display of wild emotion, her histrionics and her inability to control a runaway temper, all collided sharply with her searing ambition to emerge as the alternative face of West Bengal politics—a nemesis worthy of the over three-decade-old Marxist-led government that was in power in the state. It was a long wait, but she got there; in 2011, Mamata Banerjee formed her own government in the state.

Nothing about Mamata Banerjee's life was geared to help her cause. In a political class entrenched in prejudices of patriarchy and lineage, Mamata's lower-middle-class background, her lack of elitist accoutrements—social and educational—made her vulnerable. She more than adequately made up for all this with her careful leveraging of what the urbane would describe as the unsophisticated, jarring-to-the-ear rhetoric of the underclass. She didn't need sophisitication; Mamata had her aggression.

As she took West Bengal round a historic bend, it was clear that Mamata had become a cult personality. For more than two decades, people had watched her oscillate between shouting her tormentors down and breaking into Rabindrasangeet; braving a hail of bullets one minute and the cut of the knife another, and applying her paintbrush to the canvas the next. She is emotional to a fault, yet ruthlessly dictatorial; a people's person who could once have passed off as the queen of histrionics; a woman—single, with no rumours of romance and matrimony—without a male patron hovering in the background, or a lineage of privilege and rank rising around her like a halo. For her male adversaries, she has been a compulsive target, but not one they managed to vanquish, despite countless fierce physical assaults and cruel verbal taunts.

Mamata's politics is as riven and complex as her persona. In her books, she talks about her commitment to the ideology of humanism. But the ideological praxis Mamata has been truly committed to can be whittled down to two words: 'Combat CPI-M'. She sees no merit in the bipolar ideological/political division that the Communist Party of India (Marxist) (CPI-M), the Congress, and all their allies support: the secularism–communalism axis. Soon after breaking away from the Congress and founding the Trinamool Congress, Mamata joined the Bharatiya Janata Party (BJP)-led National Democratic Alliance (NDA) government. She was not propelled by a belief in the canons of Hindutva politics, but by her perception of the BJP as a far more committed adversary of the CPI-M than the Congress. These tactics aren't all that different from the Bahujan Samaj Party's (BSP), which has also swung from one side of the political spectrum to the other, without the ideological fetters of secularism or communalism. The BSP's moves rest purely on how much political leverage the party is able to draw from a particular alliance with the Congress, the BJP or even a third front. While many have labelled this, rather simplistically, as political opportunism, the politics behind this flexibility is more complicated than is immediately apparent. Indeed, a little later,

I will try to show why Mayawati and Mamata are comparable political personalities.

Mamata has been guided by the same logic of expediency as the BSP. After the post-Godhra pogrom in Gujarat in 2002—which the state colluded in—she claimed to have asked Atal Bihari Vajpayee to replace Gujarat Chief Minister Narendra Modi. But when that did not happen, she held her peace with the NDA. It is worth remembering that this same woman, as a member of Parliament (MP), had defied her party whip and publicly taken a belligerent stand against the Narasimha Rao government, demanding revocation of the Terrorist and Disruptive Activities (Prevention) Act (TADA).[6] Or we might recall the time she refused to speak up on behalf of Taslima Nasreen, when the Left Front government bundled the author out of Kolkata. These are incidents and events that help us to better understand Mamata and, in the course of the following chapters, I will address and elaborate on each of them.

The process of decoding Mamata Banerjee is fraught with hazards. On the one hand, there is the easy characterization: a single woman, intemperate, theatrical, riding an endless emotional roller coaster, all of which has added to her reputation as mercurial and unpredictable—a leader whom, till recently, the people of West Bengal would not trust their destiny with. Though their faith in the CPI-M had long evaporated, it was not until the Singur and Nandigram movements that the people finally turned to Mamata for succour. She endured a long wait. After all, some of the images in which she had cast herself could not be blithely waved aside. The time she danced on the bonnet of a car that was carrying the iconic socialist leader Jayaprakash Narayan to a meeting in Calcutta University; or when she flung her shawl at the former railway minister, Ram Vilas Paswan; or the time she threatened to hang herself with that famous black shawl. For years, Mamata put up a series of high-strung performances for an audience that was stunned and amused by turn. She was the grist of many harsh editorials, a source of much amusement, a cause for much hand-wringing by those who wanted a regime change in the state. As Mamata remained trapped by her own controversial, deeply conflicted personality, the CPI-M revelled in her dramatics, her idiosyncrasies—looking on with amusement at her inability to cash in on the widespread disaffection on the ground. Of course, the feud between the Congress and the Trinamool Congress further fortified the CPI-M's sense of comfort.

Undoubtedly, Mamata's failure to rein in her emotions and her shrill negativism played their part in restricting her acceptability, as did her shuffling between the Congress and the BJP, and the drama of her frequent resignation letters. But underneath the crust of outrage, indignation and blistering criticism lay strong prejudices against her class, gender and even her language of communication: the fear of the 'other' taking over political and social spaces. Mamata's lower-middle-class background, her simple sari, rubber slippers, most importantly her 'working class' syntax of communication—distinct from the sophisticated tongues that rule Bengal—came in the way of her gaining greater acceptability.

Most of the people I spoke to in the course of writing this book mentioned three qualities that impressed them the most about Mamata: her courage, simplicity and honesty. Without a doubt, the repeated and fierce attacks Mamata has suffered on her physical person seem to have rendered her fearless. From her early years as an MP in the 1980s—rushing to every volatile spot, visiting the homes of murdered Congress workers, surviving the vicious attack on her life at Kolkata's Hazra junction in the 1990s—to braving fierce assaults at Singur in 2006, Mamata was groomed, as it were, in West Bengal's school of violence. Fear she conquered, or had to, early in her combat with the CPI-M.

THE HOME AND THE WORLD

Mamata Banerjee, born on 5 January 1955, grew up in a humble home. She lived with her parents, Promileswar and Gayetri Banerjee, and six siblings at 30-B, Harish Chatterjee Street in the Kalighat area of Kolkata. That is where Mamata Banerjee, chief minister of West Bengal still lives.

A government contractor in the construction business, Promileswar died young, at the age of forty-one, leaving his family in a financial spot. Mamata was deeply attached to her father. 'When I was young, my father taught me that true humanitarianism does not differentiate between caste and creed,' Mamata writes in her autobiography.[7] She recalls how, as a young child, she would watch her father return home in a rickshaw surrounded by shopping bags. The neighbourhood children would gather and Promileswar, setting aside a bag for his family, would distribute the rest of the fruits, biscuits and lozenges among the expectant children. While her father was alive, Mamata's family lived modestly, but comfortably. According to Mamata, her father owned 'land, a house and lorries'. He was known to his neighbours as *Pandit Moshai*, and widely liked. Promileswar was an enduring influence on his daughter. 'I used to think that I would follow my father's ideals and stand by the have-nots.'[8]

Mamata has written about the sudden financial burdens that her father's death left the family with, and of the hard coping mechanisms she had to adopt to take care of her large family and very young siblings. Describing the situation as 'helpless', Mamata talks about how a few of her father's opportunistic friends, fishing in troubled waters, tried to get the family to move to their house in the Rampurhat village of Birbhum. 'At that time, all our neighbours and the members of the Block Congress stood by us and gave us strength.'[9] Mamata's eldest brother took over their father's business after the family sold their twelve bighas of land in the village.

Mamata is also emotionally close to her mother. 'Her mother, now in her eighties, is the one person who really matters to Mamata,' says Trinamool Congress MP Sudip Bandyopadhyay. 'Even today, before setting out on a journey, she asks her mother to give her ten rupees.' Mamata lives in her Kalighat home with her large family—mother, brothers, sisters-in-law, nieces and nephews. 'I stay preoccupied with politics all the time,' she writes. 'That is why the family members do not get any rest when I am in Calcutta. It is most painful when people come to me in the middle of the night or at dawn because they need some urgent help. My mother does not get the time to sleep because of this. There is no objection from them [family] in view of the nature of the work that I have taken up.'[10]

In her memoirs, Mamata writes that her childhood was a 'bit different' from that of others her age. While her friends in the ninth standard would chat and banter, Mamata would sit quietly in a corner. In class ten, while her friends planned for college, or exchanged titbits on clothes and make-up, Mamata's mind was clogged with worries. 'My mother had been unwell. I would get up at 3.30 a.m., finish the entire cooking, get my brothers and sisters ready for the day, and then somehow make it to school. Again, after school, I would rush back to cook the evening meal. When did I have the time to dream of the future?'[11]

One gets the impression that unlike her school and college friends, Mamata did not have the time to romance, or to go around with boyfriends. Or was she just dodging the temptation? It certainly sounds like she did not have the time or leisure for romance, unless it was for dolls. Mamata and her friends took the celebration of their dolls' marriages very seriously. They even ordered 'real' grocery from the neighbourhood shop. For one such wedding, Mamata ran up a tall grocery bill, getting maida, dalda, aloo and tel from the local shop. On the menu was 'dum aloo'. The Banerjee household's grocery bill overshot that month, drawing the attention of the head of the family.

Of her own association with romance, there is this rare reference in her book *Ekante* (In Solitude), the closest perhaps that Mamata came to mentioning the subject: one Bharati-di used to chaperone her on her journeys to and from Bhowanipur Girls' School. One day, Mamata had to walk back alone. Bharati-di was not well. A classmate suggested that they meet 'friends' to celebrate this sudden unexpected freedom. On their way back from school, Mamata's friends began to chat with a gaggle of boys perched on a wall around the neighbourhood park. Mamata writes that she had no idea that her friends meant to meet boys and chat with them. When she interrogated them about it, they laughingly retorted that the boys were their 'friends', their lovers! 'Hearing that, I ran breathless, all the way home. Never since did I go to school unaccompanied by Bharati-di. I could not ask anyone what "lover" meant, in case they misunderstood me or thought ill of me. Scared and keeping my thoughts to myself, I never went anywhere with my friends.'[12]

Here she comes across as deeply puritanical, keen to project the image of a sanitized, chaste womanhood, an image that India's political and social classes are comfortable with. But this image of the shrinking violet is calibrated by the image she cultivated in politics—its very converse, and one she inhabits fully. In politics, Mamata cast herself as a defiant and aggressive woman, taking the mostly male establishment head-on and getting the better of it. The question of her fractured subtextual relationship with feminism, in fact, needs more discussion, and I will get around to that in the next chapter. For the moment, let me just remark that the CPI-M's gender politics is identical to that of other parties: in their zeal for social and political transformation, the communists failed miserably vis-à-vis the gender question.

Much of the excess of Mamata's emotional rhetoric stems from a lifelong sense of betrayal. The hurt and anger run through most of her writings. In school, the classmates she helped stabbed her in the back; the party she grew up in ruined her chances of routing the CPI-M by striking undercover electoral quid pro quo deals with the communists. Haunted by a constant apprehension of persecution and conspiracy, Mamata sings a running refrain of pain and trauma. Politics is cathartic as well as traumatic for her—but this murky universe is the one she has chosen to inhabit and embrace. Her colleagues say that Mamata's lack of a personal life is, perversely, a boon for her. 'She does not have a personal life and can devote all her time to West Bengal,' a Trinamool leader told me.

A nocturnal being, Mamata keeps awake until the early hours of dawn. These days, the light burns till late in the chief minister's room in Writers' Buildings. Mamata attributes her insomniac tendencies to the near-fatal head injury she suffered in 1990, which had left her hanging on to her life by a tenuous thread. 'We have spent many sleepless nights in her MP's flat in Delhi singing Rabindrasangeet,' says Krishna Bose, MP and a founder member of the Trinamool Congress.

Mamata could do with all the hours she can get in a day, for apart from the world of politics, she has tried to make the worlds of music, painting and writing her own. How did a politician, an MP and a party president find the time to churn out some twenty-three-odd books of prose and verse? Her explanation—that she does a lot of her writing on flights—is somewhat incredible. In some of her books, she addresses her constituency, attacking the CPI-M, explaining her controversial stands on issues like Singur and Nandigram. In others, she traces her fractious relationship with her party, dwelling on her years of growing up, her struggle and her family. *Andolan*, published in 2009, compiles Mamata's thoughts, primarily on Nandigram, Singur, the Rizwanur Rehman case,[13] CPI-M orchestrated terror and what she calls 'police raj'. *Struggle for Existence* (1998) and *Ekante* (2003) are deeply personal and political. *Trinamool* (2010) is a dramatic account of conspiracies and counter-conspiracies leading to the formation of the Trinamool Congress.

The most remarkable thing she carries from her own modest background into her books is an instinctive empathy for the poor. She did not need to strain herself to connect with the people at the grass roots, who were her fans long before the middle class and the elite were willing to get on board with her.

The Context

I am deliberately avoiding the easy temptation to straitjacket Mamata Banerjee within a grid of binaries—mature/immature, emotional/pragmatic, rational/irrational, pro- and anti-industry. I will try, instead, to capture something of her tangled and complex personality. An understanding of her, as I have said, must be mediated by considerations of class, gender, language, as well as the political and non-political methods used by her adversaries in their battles with her. Without these, one might conflate Mamata with her histrionics.

The literature she authored is an important insight into how the Trinamool chief perceives herself in relation to her family, the parties she has aligned with, her notion of politics, path-breaking movements like Singur and Nandigram, and the culture of West Bengal. She articulates the relationship between the personal and the political through the shrill language of pain, trauma and victimhood, all drenched in drama. But these anguished outpourings and high-pitched exhortations take on deeper shades of meaning within the wider context—personal, social, political—which cradled and nurtured Mamata.

I have tried to capture some of the layers that heightened Mamata's emotional, dramatic impulses, her paranoia about persecution and conspiracies. Some of these are interpreted through the lens of gender, her lower-middle-class background and her use of language of communication, which both caught popular imagination and offended the elite.

Perhaps it is equally helpful to locate Mamata's emergence within a broader frame of cultural changes: the disintegration of bhadralok aesthetics, and the emergence of a fragmented cultural patois. Cultural theorist Moinak Biswas posed this question: 'Does the bhadra circle exist in the same form any more?' Arpita Ghosh, theatre director, told me that the definition of bhadralok has been bequeathed to us by the Left: 'The Left has defined bhadralok for us. Bhadraloks are supposed to exercise restraint, behave, talk, and even conduct their agitations in a certain manner.' In a more historical context, the Bengali bhadralok has had an anti-establishment edge since the colonial days. Even before the Marxists came to power in 1977, a large section of their leadership originated precisely from this anti-establishment bhadralok culture.

As opposed to this educated elite Left leadership, the Trinamool is headed by a leader, apparently with 'no culture', little restraint, speaking the language of the underclass, lacking the resonance of the bhadralok-speak. I will also look at the irony of a situation where Mamata tends to get cast as dangerous, a class-other, who does not know the art of governance—all charges hurled in the 1960s and 1970s at the communists before they came to power.

The Mamata mystique is as much cultural as political and social. Her political assertion coincides with the larger transformations that have taken place in the worlds of media, communication, music and culture. These are spaces where the vernacular has retreated, making way for a hybrid language, a mix of Bengali, English and even Hindi, and an equally hybrid representation of cultural forms. 'The bhadralok subject in question hardly has any scope for lament if it has decided to abandon its vernacular. It could be worthwhile to look for the shifts in communication, pedagogy and artistic production,' suggests Biswas.[14]

The very idea that politics, in a democratic nation, is about representing the masses was becoming contentious now. A few years ago, political actors in West Bengal were confident of their constituencies. This confidence faded with the disenchantment of the people with the Left Front and the rise of Mamata Banerjee as a figure who does not stand for anything that the urban middle class can easily understand. This partly explains why Mamata and the Trinamool elicit such varied reactions, even from within the Left. While the CPI-M and its allies would like us to believe she is a right-wing fascist, other shades of Leftists characterize her as a populist without ideological commitments. Others still, including many who were formerly part of various factions of Marxist–Leninist parties, see in Mamata the only viable, popular alternative to the Left Front. These varying opinions illustrate just how unstable the political situation in West Bengal is, where no party can any longer claim the 'masses' as theirs.

Biswas believes that this is part of a much larger two-pronged cultural shift. On one hand, the Trinamool adopts an older, elite Leftist idiom in its style of politics—its rhetoric favouring the underclass—and its cultural appropriation of Left-radical traditions, like the songs of the Indian People's Theatre Association (IPTA). On the other hand, in recent years, West Bengal has seen the emergence of forms of culture that seriously undermine bhadralok dominance, putting this older order in a crisis. Biswas argues: 'The territory of the image is giving in to unfamiliar people seeking entry. Those who find it wholly unacceptable are likely to turn away from all politics. But the signs are clear that the minority culture of distinction has opened its doors to other semiotic neighbourhoods, and has even become dependent on the invasions for survival.'[15]

These changing forms of cultural, artistic, linguistic representations are, in a sense, emblematic of the disintegration of a pristine, unadulterated bhadralok culture. Biswas takes the example of Durga Puja to argue how the festival's changing forms have created an entirely new kind of public art. The form of this celebration has diversified and altered over the last decade or so, crystallizing in a hybrid synthesis of academic fine arts, folk craft traditions, traditional art practices and new media elements. Contemporary Bengali pop and the rock bands mushrooming in Bengal convey the changing syntax of the Bengali language; television shows as well as media articles are increasingly using this 'non-bhadralok' language of nonchalant irreverence. The popular cultural idioms in West Bengal have changed drastically enough in the last decade or so to break down the quintessential Bengali bhadralok's resistance to less gentrified representations of art, music and culture. Contemporary Bengali authors like Nabarun Bhattacharya and film director Anjan Dutta manifest this changing cultural idiom in their work.[16]

Superstition and Spirituality

Mamata has a firm, unabashed belief in the supernatural. Not surprising, given her frequent encounters with vicious political violence, and escaping death by a whisker. It must have made her survival seem nothing short of a divine marvel, a miracle of sorts. She has sought and derived much of her strength from her belief in the power of divine interventions. Among the many incidents narrated in *Ekante*, here's one that testifies to her belief in the magical manifestation of the supernatural:

'I had not gone to Tarapith for quite some time. It was in Delhi that I dreamt that I was offering puja there. On waking up I started thinking of making a trip. Returning to Kolkata I told my mother about the dream. She said a few days earlier an old woman had suddenly showed up at our house. And this woman too before disappearing said, "Ask your daughter to go to Tarapith."'[17] Her dream and the old woman's appearance, Mamata felt sure, were conveying a message. Needless to say, she went to Tarapith as soon as she could arrange it.[18]

More recently, she is known to have said that the year 2001 went badly for her—her party fared poorly in the West Bengal assembly polls—because she could not manage to make it to the Kalighat temple's annual puja that year. Her sparse, austere 8ft x 6ft bedroom at Kalighat has a prominent photograph of Kali. Trinamool Bhawan, the party's headquarters, bears the imprint of a similar kind of religiosity. On the first floor landing of the Bhawan hangs a large photograph of Mamata's favourite deity.

'Mamata Banerjee is not strictly a rationalist,' Saugata Roy, Central minister and Trinamool Congress leader, told me in an interview. In fact, her art of political communication draws heavily from the works and styles of religious leaders like Ramakrishna Paramahansa and Vivekananda. Her references are laced with quotations from religious scriptures. In *Ekante*, Mamata writes of a number of incidents that bear testimony to her faith in supernatural wonders and divine interventions. Logic is not important here, faith is. Her family started worshipping Kali from 1979, she writes. Apparently, the goddess appeared in her brother's dream, reprimanding him for not worshipping her and selling her clay images instead. The dream sent the brother into a delirium of sorts that he came out of only after promising to worship Kali. This is how the Kali puja tradition started at Mamata's residence. In her book, she devotes page after page to her supernatural experiences, her visits to Belur Math, the headquarters of the Ramakrishna Mission, her dreams in which goddesses make their appearances, her constant encounters with this shadowy world of divinity. Here is Mamata's own account of one such incident:

> I vividly recall one incident. Ratan-da [Ratan Mukherjee], my personal secretary in Delhi, had gone to Bangalore with his wife Moloya for their daughter Pablo's education. On his return, he gifted me a small sandalwood figurine of the Buddha. My rooms both in Kolkata and Delhi have only books and cassettes as decorations. Photographs and idols of gods and goddesses I worship, as well as a shawl from Ajmer Sharif, are always with me. I kept the small figurine of the Buddha next to one of my cassettes. One day I was writing when a colleague came into the room and said, 'Didi, give me one of your deities.' I told her, 'Take whichever you want.' She reached out for the Buddha figurine, but couldn't lift it, not even after putting pressure. I said, 'How can you not lift it—it's a sandalwood statue, extremely light.' She replied, 'I am not able to move it at all.' I thought to myself how that could be. I had just now lifted it. Had it turned to stone? My colleague said, 'Didi, the deity doesn't want to come to me.' I told her, 'Maybe, but then you will not be able to take the idol…'[19]

These stories give us a glimpse into the rationally impenetrable world of faith and belief that Mamata comfortably inhabits. She has an explanation for all her supernatural encounters: 'Without weighing it on the scales of polemics, I have realized that people have a deep faith in the deities they worship. Unlike in a polemical debate, there are no mathematical or logical deductions, but only what we traditionally describe as spiritualism is born out of this belief.'[20] This deep faith leads her to believe that providential intervention saved her life in the bloody attack at Hazra junction in 1990. How else, she asks, could she have lifted her hands and shielded her head even as she was brutally attacked; her instinctive gesture at that critical moment prevented the blows from splitting open her head.

Mamata's curious mixture of the religious, the superstitious and the political find wider resonance in the transformation of cultural spaces that were till recently hegemonized by the Marxists and the bhadralok.

The Trinamool Congress chief is popularizing a new political language, the very antithesis of the Marxist lingua franca. Since Ramakrishna Paramahansa has been an abiding influence on her life, influencing her vocabulary greatly, it may be interesting to look at his emergence as a cult figure, his acceptance among the Bengali bhadralok, and the essence of his philosophy. It would also be important to locate Mamata in the broad Ramakrishna–Vivekananda tradition to understand the connection between contemporary social, political and cultural transformations and her acceptance among large sections of Bengali bhadralok.

According to historian Sumit Sarkar, *Kathamrita*, the text claiming to contain conversations with Ramakrishna between February 1882 and August 1886 was the product of a 'liminal' moment, which was witness to 'the rustic Brahman becoming the guru of the city bhadralok, the latter falling under the spell of an idiom, values, personality very different from their own'.[21] The quintessential Bengali bhadralok of nineteenth-century colonial Bengal, stifled with the boredom of his clerical job, was drawn to Ramakrishna's style of communication, which worked through parables rather than the invocation of pure, logical arguments. The Bengali bhadralok partly 'constructed' Ramakrishna to cope with his increasing feeling of alienation with contemporary life.

'There was little obviously new in Ramakrishna's teachings. That may have been one of his strengths, for through Ramakrishna, the city bhadralok could be imagining themselves to be reaching back to lost traditional moorings in the countryside, in simple faith conveyed through rustic language,' Sarkar writes.[22] It is not difficult to locate echoes of Mamata Banerjee in this description; or to see why the figure of Ramakrishna might have resonance for Mamata.

It is true that the Ramakrishna heritage has by now been appropriated by several constituencies and separated by class, profession as well as time. By the twentieth century, the ambience of the world inhabited by clerics in nineteenth-century colonial Bengal was transformed by strikes and the growth of Left trade unions. But the appeal of Ramakrishna had travelled beyond the offices at Dalhousie Square. Large sections of the social elite of Kolkata had become loyal devotees of the guru. Such was the sweep of his philosophy that it even drew within its fold revolutionary terrorists of the national movement. For instance, Sumit Sarkar mentions the two accused in the Alipur bomb case of 1908, who along with others 'sought shelter within the Ramakrishna Mission in the wake of political frustration and failure'.[23] The Left Front government too, despite its atheism, had strong linkages with the Ramakrishna Mission, particularly its social service networks.

Still, given the growing crisis in bhadralok culture, these settled meanings of the figure of Ramakrishna can once again become unsettled. Some of this is in evidence in Mamata's political rhetoric. Faith and not 'rationality' is what moves Mamata. Her faith lies in a normative understanding of universal love, brotherhood, equality, peace. It is not that the Trinamool Congress chief is not conscious of the divisive, discriminatory implications of class and caste, but her world view is not complicated by the pull and push of class struggle, of movements of caste assertion and the like. She places her faith instead on principles of universal goodness, love, peace and harmony, which she believes will redress the ills in society and the world at large. Even her logical inferences are couched in popular parables and simple, uncomplicated metaphors.

Ramakrishna imbibed his central message from bhakti (devotion) rather than from textual exegesis. For Mamata, manashram (mental labour) and lived experience are as important as, if not more than, text-based learning.

Her books too draw their content from her own experiences and of those around her; little attempt is made to make wider political, social or cultural intersections. In Mamata's political career, Singur and Nandigram were aberrations, catapulting her to a position of political ascendancy. Thus far, she was not a leader born out of a movement, nor did she express faith in any particular movement. Her books, in fact, repeatedly stress the significance of faith. 'It is faith which imbues humans with devotion, which in turn provides strength, empowering them. Human strength is expressed through the spirit of service made to humanity,' she writes.[24]

If she draws on Ramakrishna's faith-based language, the

spirit of service running through Mamata's writings seems to be inspired by Vivekananda rather than Ramakrishna, who showed little or no interest in philanthropy. It was Vivekananda who popularized organized philanthropy through the concept of daridranarayan (the poor representing God).

What Mamata has done politically is to bring Ramakrishna and Vivekananda into her rhetoric and discourse. There can be no denying Mamata's intrinsic tendency to convey politics through the idioms of ordinary life: that is as integral to her style of communication as is her slogan 'Maa, Maati, Manush' (mother, land, people). But by peppering her political speeches with frequent references to the philosophy of Ramakrishna and Vivekananda, whether with regard to the principle of humanism, the ethos of social service or even long-forgotten work ethic, Mamata has done more than merely utilize rhetoric. She has also tried to bring these influences into the realm of policy and administration.

The slew of projects that Mamata undertook as railway minister to help the temples and institutions built in Ramakrishna's name is a prominent signifier of her strong ties with the guru. The Trinamool Congress–run Kolkata Municipal Corporation (KMC) is engaged in renovating Mayer Bari (mother's house), where Ramakrishna's wife Sarada Devi lived, and its surrounding areas at Bagbazar Street. On 23 May 1909, Sarada Devi first stepped inside the building where she lived in virtual anonymity until her death on 20 July 1920. The Kolkata Municipal Corporation plans to overhaul the entire building which is included in the list of the city's heritage sites. The KMC also plans to renovate the Kashi Mitra burning ghat, now a refuge of 'antisocials', where Ramakrishna's last rites were performed in 1886. Plans are under way to demolish the unauthorized structures that have come up there in the last decade, besides sprucing up the memorial built in memory of Ramakrishna.

In January 2010, the railway minister laid the foundation stone of a ₹600-crore Kolkata Metro Railway extension project from Dum Dum to Dakshineswar, housing the famous Kali temple associated with Ramakrishna. The following year, in January, she flagged off a special exhibition train, Vivekananda Express, showcasing the life and philosophy of the spiritual leader. The monks at Belur Math have described Mamata as the 'new hope' of West Bengal. In February 2011, she dedicated a car-parking facility, a rail link to Belur and a multifunctional complex to the headquarters of the Ramakrishna Math and Mission. 'Developing a car park is not the job of the railways. But I am listening to my heart and setting aside the technical problems,' Mamata claimed.

In the run-up to the 2011 assembly elections, Mamata Banerjee was preparing in earnest for her new role. She was attempting to reinvent her image from a partisan, no-holds-barred, fierce combatant to that of a mature, responsible chief ministerial candidate. Her tone was now tempered and decisions more sober, less on the spur of the moment. But the process of transition did not affect Mamata's language of political and cultural invocation, which continued to rely as heavily as before on her spiritual gurus. And her voters seemed to like it.

2

From Jadavpur to Delhi

The 1989 general elections—in which Mamata Banerjee lost from Kolkata's Jadavpur constituency—were a turning point. Her trips to Delhi became increasingly infrequent after this. The Congress activist was vanquished that year, but she was then doubly determined to jolt, if not topple, the mighty Left Front government. Mamata plunged headlong into agitations in her home state.

The Left Front government by then was more than a decade old and was comfortably ensconced in Writers' Buildings.[1] In 1990, street protests against a hike in bus fares peaked in Kolkata; three people died in police firing. The Congress announced a general strike on 16 August. In the midst of this political turbulence, Congress leader Rajiv Gandhi summoned Mamata to Delhi. Reluctant yet unable to turn down her mentor's call, Mamata agreed to go, but she told Rajiv's personal secretary Vincent George that she needed to return to Kolkata the same day. In Delhi, Mamata headed straight for the Congress office, where Rajiv Gandhi cautioned her that her life was in danger. He asked if he could provide her with any assistance at this critical hour. Overwhelmed, Mamata said she simply wanted his blessings.

Rajiv's warning was borne out in the ghoulish drama at Hazra junction on 16 August 1990, the day of the general strike. The brutal attack on Mamata that day was the worst yet of a life marked by violence and struggle. I will discuss the attack in detail a little later, because it's crucial to understanding Mamata—for it served to cement her perception of herself as a perennial victim in West Bengal politics.

Climbing Mount Improbable

But first I need to step back into the stormy 1970s, when Mamata stepped into the realm of active politics, before the Left Front came to power. This is where the story of her 'victimhood' really begins. Political violence was then at an all-time high. The Naxal movement[2] had exploded in 1967, shaking up urban Kolkata in its wake. The Congress government in Bengal brutally repressed the Naxalites. This was also the time when the CPI-M was a pariah, fighting from the underground until it came to power emphatically in 1977. But West Bengal's culture of negotiating politics through violence did not disappear with the rise of the parliamentary Left. It merely transformed with the establishment of the new epoch of the Left Front in West Bengal. By the time Mamata broke away from the Congress, and the Trinamool Congress was born, this culture of violent political brinkmanship was all the state knew.

Indeed, the Left's need to leverage violence against an effete Opposition is baffling. Why did the CPI-M work up such a sweat over Mamata Banerjee after the Left had decimated the

Congress so effectively? Why did the party constantly target the Opposition leader when it had reaped spectacular mileage out of the Congress's perennial factional feuds—not only by coming to power in 1977, but by continuing to hold on for the following three decades?

Mamata Banerjee entered politics in 1970. As an undergraduate in Kolkata's Jogamaya Devi College, she became active in the Chhatra Parishad (CP), the Congress's students wing. The college union was then controlled by the Democratic Socialist Organization (DSO), students wing of the Socialist Unity Centre of India (SUCI). Mamata soon started a parallel Chhatra Parishad union, launching her career as a political activist. Jogamaya Devi College became the first site of her intense engagement with politics. In her autobiography, Mamata writes, 'From 1972 to 1977, West Bengal had a Congress government. Many had offered me jobs. I did not take up any job because that would not have given me time for politics.'[3] Her dogged fight against the DSO drew the attention of some Congress leaders, even though she didn't really know them personally then. In those days, Kolkata was on the boil; educational institutions had virtually ground to a halt and classes were regularly suspended following pitched battles between the Chhatra Parishad and the CPI-M's Students Federation of India (SFI). Through this period of unrest, Mamata completed her master's and BEd and LLB. But her future in politics was already chalked out.

'I still remember the day I entered active politics. The feeling of exultation, the intention to do endless work, the idealism,' Mamata writes.[4] If she had any niggling doubts about her true calling, they were put to rest by the mad rush of adrenaline that coursed through her veins as she hit the streets in her political campaigns and demonstrations during those heady yet dangerous days of student politics. Mamata was out on Kolkata's streets defending Indira Gandhi after the latter lost the parliamentary elections. She was at the forefront of agitations led by Subrata Mukherjee, then a Congress legislator. From waving black flags at then prime minister Morarji Desai on his visit to Kolkata to getting into a bloody fight with the Left student activists in Ashutosh College, she was gaining a reputation for being a strong combatant of the CPI-M.

In her autobiography, Mamata seeks to dispel the myth that it was Subrata Mukherjee who introduced her to politics, but she does credit other Congressmen for it. 'Many people think that Subrata-da inducted me into politics. But this is not correct. I entered active politics in 1970. At that time, the persons who had helped me most were Partha Roy Chowdhury [current president of the South Calcutta District Committee], Ranjit Ghosh, Rana-da [the then general secretary of the Block Congress Committee] and Dilip Majumdar [now a councillor of the Calcutta Municipal Corporation and a borough chairman].'[5]

But during the formative years of her political career, Subrata Mukherjee was indeed among Mamata's mentors. Later, their relationship soured, and Mamata describes her one-time mentor as a 'tarmuj' (watermelon)—her label for Congress leaders she suspected of swinging underhand electoral deals with the CPI-M. Like the colours of a watermelon, green on the outside and red inside, these Congress leaders, despite their public allegiance to the party, or so Mamata believed, were in cohorts with the CPI-M—they were plotting to keep the Left Front government safe.

Brilliant and acidic as that description may be, there is no denying that Mamata spent a substantial slice of her initial political life as an apprentice to Subrata Mukherjee. On his part, Mukherjee does not claim to have brought Mamata into politics. 'As a student of Jogamaya Devi College, Mamata was actively involved with the Chhatra Parishad. Later we worked closely in the INTUC [Indian National Trade Union Congress]. I made her the INTUC secretary and sent her to Malaysia for training. Mamata became an effective leader,' he told me in an interview. Mukherjee encouraged the young and enthusiastic activist to 'do everything', from organizing INTUC state conferences to delivering speeches. 'Those days, women leaders with oratorical skills were hard to find. Mamata was one of those rare finds. She would travel from district to district delivering speeches.'

Prabir Ghosal, senior journalist with the *Bartamaan* newspaper, recollects the first time he met Mamata in the INTUC office: 'As I was walking up the stairs, I could hear someone making a speech. Peeping into the room, I saw this slim, young girl. Stopping in the middle of her speech, she asked if I was looking for someone. That was Mamata Banerjee.' She was heady with the thrill of activism.

After winning the 1977 assembly elections, the Left Front had taken charge of Writers' Buildings. A badly mauled Congress was in no position to rustle up even a semblance of a political and electoral challenge to the Left Front. In the 1984 elections, the Congress seemed to have recovered somewhat, but it was only a sudden surge of sympathy following Indira Gandhi's assassination. Though a one-time electoral gain for the Congress, for Mamata, the polls were a career-turner.

Prior to 1984, the idea that this political greenhorn, this hot-headed activist could trounce veteran Left leader Somnath Chatterjee in the CPI-M's very own Jadavpur constituency would have sounded like the blather of an impractical optimist. But that is just what happened. Mamata would have attributed her stunning victory to the writ of destiny, pre-ordained and immutable. But not even her staunch faith could have prepared her for this radical turn in her career.

Ironically enough, the idea of fielding Mamata in a CPI-M stronghold was not a strategic decision. It was a spur-of-the-moment resolution, driven by the Congress's lack of strength and dearth of active workers, particularly of women activist-orators. Mamata seemed to fill the void. No one expected her to deliver such an extraordinary result. Here is Subrata Mukherjee's account of how Mamata was catapulted into the eye of sudden fame: 'The elections were approaching. Indira-ji suddenly asked me to find a woman candidate. The Congress was in a bad shape. Finding women candidates was a tough job. I suggested Mamata's name, and she got her nomination from the Jadavpur constituency.' If Mamata's nomination had taken political circles by surprise, her victory literally took their breath away. The first-time MP was just twenty-nine years old.

'Undoubtedly, the assassination of Indira Gandhi was a factor, but it was humiliating for Somnath Chatterjee, almost an institution in electoral politics, to be defeated by such a young political novice,' Subrata Mukherjee said. And Somnath Chatterjee did indeed smart. In his autobiography, *Keeping the Faith*, he writes, 'I stood for the election from Jadavpur in Calcutta, but was unsuccessful, primarily because of the sympathy wave for the Congress. Without in any way giving an excuse, I would like to mention the sustained campaign of vilification unleashed against me on totally concocted allegations and misrepresentation. I had never before faced such slander and nor would I do so in any other election thereafter.'[6] He then goes on to add: 'I acknowledged my defeat and I believe I was the first person to congratulate Mamata Banerjee, to whom I had lost by less than 20,000 votes.'

Chatterjee's observation, more than two decades later, that the 'vilification' campaign in 1984, presumably by Banerjee, was unlike any other he had faced underlines the animus between the two leaders. 'If Chatterjee is alleging a vilification campaign, I would say Mamata Banerjee too was a victim of vilification,' retorts Mukherjee, referring to the campaign drummed up by the Left about Mamata's 'non-existent' PhD from the US-based East Georgia University. Apparently, the university, though it exists, was not empowered to grant PhDs. But back in 1984, the whole of West Bengal, particularly Kolkata, was agog with speculations about Mamata's 'fake' degree. Years later, talking about the campaign, Mamata said the viciousness of it made her feel like an unlettered woman, despite her degrees in education and law.

Mamata watchers believe that her astounding victory from Jadavpur opened to her a space waiting to be occupied: an Opposition leader who was ambitious, even reckless and flamboyant. After the Left Front's victory, the Congress had wilted into near-non-existence. Stepping into this vacuum, Mamata cast herself in the image of a relentless fighter who could stake claim to power in the state. She tried to transfer to the moribund party her abundant energy and passion. 'Mamata Banerjee functions with a self-styled imagination,' says Trinamool Congress MP Sudip Bandyopadhyay. No textbook lessons, no rule books. Impulse, anger and a passion for justice were the key words in the newly elected MP's political vocabulary.

Krishna Bose, a founder member of the Trinamool Congress, recalls Mamata as a tireless campaigner during the 1984 elections. But Mamata was not new to campaigning. She had campaigned for Krishna's husband, Sisir Bose, in the 1982 assembly elections. 'Both of us did door-to-door campaigning in the multistoreyed apartments of the Chowringhee constituency. I remember we would take the lift, ring doorbells to the flats on both sides of the landing, then take the stairs down,' Krishna said. The summer heat was killing. 'But Mamata was debating whether we should carry umbrellas, about how it may be perceived by the ordinary people. She would tell Sisir Bose not to reveal discomfort, even if he did experience any while campaigning in the slums.' By the end of the campaign, the Bose couple had grown extremely fond of Mamata. Sisir was probably the first to introduce Mamata to Rajiv Gandhi, who later backed her at every stage. 'It was at Netaji Bhavan in this room that Sisir Bose introduced Mamata to Rajiv Gandhi when he was in Kolkata for the AICC session in 1983. We were all in this room. Sisir introduced Mamata to Rajiv as a "very good worker". Later Mamata thanked Dr Bose saying nobody else would have been so generous,' Krishna told me when we met at Netaji Bhavan.

Though Krishna Bose was not very active in the Trinamool Congress's campaign in the run-up to the 2011 assembly elections, Mamata has not forgotten their years of hard toil or their late-night soirees of Rabindrasangeet in her MP's flat in Delhi. A near-insomniac, Mamata would complain that Krishna had fallen asleep at midnight, and not stayed up to sing that one particular Rabindrasangeet she had so wanted to hear. 'Even today, when I go to Delhi, Mamata insists I stay in one of their MP's flats. She tells me, "We have so many MPs now. You must stay at our place,"' Krishna said. Mamata also always remembers Krishna on her birthday. 'Even this year [2010], on 26 December, Mamata landed up at my place, gifted me a shawl.'

Mamata's unexpected victory in 1984 put her firmly on a militant path. She began touring districts across the length and breadth of West Bengal. The Congress's unexpected electoral gains (sixteen seats, even if it was only because of the sympathy wave) raised the CPI-M's hackles. The enemy it had axed so thoroughly in 1977 seemed to have risen. The paranoid Left believed that the tide had begun to turn again. It had been fighting the Congress for most of its political life, and so was, of course, just waiting for the Congress to strike back. The CPI-M could not have anticipated that it would stay at the crease for thirty-four years.

To stop what it perceived as the Congress's resurgence, the party ratcheted up violence. It unleashed terror in villages across West Bengal, attacking Congress workers. This was the scene Mamata entered, flush with the success of her maiden electoral victory. Prabir Ghosal recalls that she would rush to wherever Congress workers were attacked or killed. She had courted danger right from her days as a student activist. The first in a series of trips Mamata made in this period was to Magrahat in South 24 Parganas, where a Congress worker was brutally murdered and his wife gang-raped by alleged antisocials backed by the CPI-M. Media reports spoke of the horror of the incident—the assailants 'playing football' with the murdered worker's severed head. Mamata's visit and her meeting with the family of the deceased made front-page news. Across the state, the Congress MP reached every combat zone, lending a shoulder to every grieving family, commiserating with them as 'Didi': the elder sister, their leader, confidante and companion.

The image of Didi, a 'people's person'—renowned Bengali writer Mahasweta Devi's description of Mamata—gained flesh and blood roughly between 1985 and 1990. Mamata's personal contact with people at the grass roots, her intimate knowledge of their problems, the warmth and candour of her engagement with them lent to the young leader a rarefied quality. In a way, she humanized political engagement; people took to her ordinariness, her earthy language, bare of the refined syntax other politicians used. The CPI-M, which used to be the party with an ear to the ground, was now constructing a huge, unassailable, dehumanized party apparatus.

'In her first term as an MP, Mamata built her image of a resolute adversary of the CPI-M, a fearless public protester,' claims Saugata Roy, senior Trinamool Congress leader and minister in the current United Progressive Alliance (UPA) government. He recalls Mamata camping in Himachal Pradesh for a fortnight to get back the bodies of trekkers who had lost their lives on an expedition. They were from her constituency. 'The media zeroed in on her. No longer subservient to Subrata Mukherjee, Mamata Banerjee came into her own.' During this period, Mamata, a Congress MP, echoed the Left's protests that the Centre's freight equalization policy was hurting West Bengal. She put her own government on the mat for delaying sanction to the Haldia Petrochemical project.

Mamata's Congress Complex

The second big landmark of Mamata's political career was the assassination of Rajiv Gandhi in 1991—an event she has repeatedly referred to, even in 2011, after the assembly elections, in which she finally dislodged the Left Front from power. 'Since my father's death, this was the second time that I was left without a guardian. I could not speak to anyone for seven days. I could not eat. I closed the door of my room and just wept,' she recalls.[7] In spite of opposition from party colleagues, Rajiv Gandhi had appointed Mamata president of the West Bengal Youth Congress—the first of several career-turners in Mamata's political life. As Youth Congress president, she got the space she wanted for mobilizing Congress activists and drumming up militant, noisy protests. 'Mamata later formed the Trinamool Congress mainly with the members of the Youth Congress,' Subrata Mukherjee contends.

Rajiv Gandhi's sudden death left Mamata to battle her many detractors single-handedly. The state Congress leaders sullenly watched Mamata's appeal grow among the people as her raucous yet distinctive oratorical style struck a chord, and her undoubted ability to make a 'connection' with people endeared her to her vote bank.

In Delhi, the Congress's top leaders were aware that the sparring factions of the West Bengal units were haemorrhaging the party. 'In the 1980s, Indira Gandhi told Sisir Bose that it was impossible to find out who was fighting whom in the West Bengal unit,' Krishna Bose said. Not that this was unique to West Bengal; Congress state units across the country were riddled with conspiracies and factional strife. 'In West Bengal, as in many other states, factional fights within the Congress usually pitted the organizational wing of the party against the younger energetic workers of the party, the so-called opposition between the conservative and the radical elements,' argues political scientist Dwaipayan Bhattacharyya.[8]

Even though the local leaders were pitted against each other, they owed absolute loyalty to the Gandhi-Nehru family—then Indira and Rajiv, now Sonia and Rahul. In Congress politics, the survival and prominence of its leaders eventually hinges on one axis: benediction of the 'dynasty'. Deference and unqualified subservience to the 'family' are essential prerequisites to playing an active and vital role in the party. For a while, Mamata had Rajiv Gandhi on her side and this lent her more than a modicum of immunity. Perhaps in recognition of her association with Rajiv, to date, Mamata seems to have a special place in her heart for his widow.

However, Mamata formed the Trinamool Congress against Sonia's explicit desire not to split the party. She knew that, if she were not to cut the umbilical cord, her political ambitions would be reduced to a naught, and her combat mission against the Left Front government, doomed.

A splintered Opposition, exhausting its energies fighting itself, was a boon for the Left Front government and the CPI-M specifically, guaranteeing its amazing political longevity. After a decade or so in the Writers' Buildings, the Left Front had started moving away from its ideological axis; there was escalating disaffection among the people. But the Congress was simply not in a position to draw electoral or political dividends from the situation. The low index of Opposition unity can be gauged from the fact that even though long before the Left Front's 2009 electoral debacle in the Lok Sabha polls, much of the electorate in West Bengal had become tired of the CPI-M, neither Opposition party managed to dislodge it from power. A large part of the CPI-M's phenomenal victories was contingent upon keeping the Opposition split, so they would cut into each other's anti-Left vote bank.

An impatient Mamata was straining for a no-holds-barred fight against the Marxist dispensation. She sniffed conspiracy in the dark corners of back rooms where deals were swung and manipulative strategies were put in place. Mamata strongly suspected a section of the Congress was conniving with the CPI-M, especially around election time, when quid-pro-quo deals were being discussed and finalized. To Mamata, her fight against the Left Front government appeared to be hers and hers alone. In the wake of the Bofors scam, and a rising anti-Congress wave in the 1989 general elections, Mamata lost the Jadavpur seat—though some attribute her defeat to a Congress–CPI-M conspiracy. In the 1991 polls, Mamata bounced back, changing her seat and winning from South Kolkata.

A new phase began when Prime Minister Narasimha Rao inducted Mamata into his government as the minister of state, Human Resources Development, including Youth Affairs, Sports, Women and Child Development. The volatile Mamata hardly fit the description of an obedient, disciplined member of the council of ministers. As a senior Trinamool leader pointed out to me, Mamata Banerjee was always a 'contrarian'. Her inclination to strike out on her own, regardless of the party line, came to the fore during her first ministerial term itself. In her autobiographical narrative, she does not shy away from regaling the reader with vivid accounts of the means she adopted to achieve her ends.

During the tenure of the Rao government, in 1995, Mamata's continued and forceful demands for revoking TADA raised a storm within and outside her own party. Realizing that the Congress did not want her to bring up the issue in the Lok Sabha, Mamata decided to settle the matter her own way. 'After considering all aspects, I made a small placard to carry to the

Parliament, though I knew this was not permissible. Since I was not getting a chance to speak, this was the only alternative. Written on the placard were two words TA-TA to TADA,' she writes.[9] Trite as they were, the two words had the desired effect. Perhaps unaware of Mamata's fiercely stubborn and defiant streak, Parliamentary Affairs Minister V.C. Shukla pulled her up for this. Sure enough, Mamata only scaled up her protests.

Challenging her party both at home and in Delhi was routine for Mamata, almost as much as a dharna or a fast was for her. She even refused to campaign for the party in the panchayat elections of 1993 and the municipal elections of 1995, or to participate in the Bengal bandh organized by the West Bengal Pradesh Congress Committee. In 1997, the revelations of the Jain Commission report, which pointed a finger at the Dravida Munnetra Kazhagam (DMK) in the assassination of Rajiv Gandhi, triggered political instability at the Centre. The fate of the Congress-backed United Front government, of which DMK was a constituent, hung by a thread. Mamata predictably went into a tizzy, especially because the controversy centred on the death of Rajiv Gandhi. Agitated that the Congress Parliamentary Party was not bringing a no-confidence motion against the I.K. Gujral government, she decided to submit the motion herself. 'Then began the "hot and cold" intimidations,' Mamata writes. 'At first, Congress leaders began telephoning me to convince me not to press ahead with the motion, then they graduated to outright third-degree police methods.'[10] Mamata, of course, refused to budge.

She was more than just a contrarian, as her party colleagues call her; Mamata had a problem submitting to authority. She refused to be bound by the rules within which members of a political party usually function. Each time she clashed with her party—over TADA, the Jain Commission report, the bifurcation of Eastern Railways—she grounded her defiance in lofty idealism, in the rhetoric of ethics, her conscience, human rights, protection of minorities and West Bengal's interests. She freely quotes Rabindranath Tagore and Vivekananda to defend her defiance: 'It is true that I was a member of the ruling party, but what about my conscience? That was not mortgaged to any party. The efforts of my party colleagues for my election deserve to be acknowledged, but what is more important to me are the people who elected me as a member of Parliament.'[11]

This was her attitude right through her time with the Congress and later with the NDA. But as supreme leader of her own party, she metamorphosed from an activist who shrugged off party discipline to the dictator-like president of the Trinamool Congress. The spat between her and musician-turned-MP Kabir Suman in 2010 underscored this authoritarian streak. She refused to concede to the artist the autonomous space she had fought so stubbornly for in her own political career. It is possible to argue that her regard for a party line and discipline was symptomatic of her maturity, the transition she has made since the 1990s. But one could also argue that what manifests as dictatorship is substantially the same as her earlier defiance. Mamata is now—as she was back then—someone who believes herself to be in the right, who trusts her way as the only one worth following. I will get back to this at greater length, but first we must return to the 1990s.

Mamata's dramatic resignations in that decade seem to fortify her image as an unstable and unreliable leader—as someone who would invariably strike out on her own. It was a perception that damaged her image and hurt her political ambitions.

While the first-time minister did take her job seriously in the one year and five months she shepherded the Ministry of Human Resource Development in the Narasimha Rao government, she also continued to publicly express her differences of opinion with the ruling establishment. She began by questioning the government why it did not treat sports and youth welfare as subjects of national concern or interest. Then, she moved on to the TADA protests, a far more inflammable subject than sports and youth affairs.

One of Mamata's most audacious moves came in 1992. From the heart of Kolkata, during a public rally at the Brigade Parade grounds on 25 November, Mamata announced her resignation from the Union ministry. Grounding her sudden resignation in 'Bengal vs Centre' rhetoric, Mamata argued that she needed to stay in West Bengal. Her ministerial berth, she said, was a gift from the people which she laid down at the 'doors of the people's court'. The government accepted her resignation in January 1993.

Two years later, Mamata shot off yet another resignation letter—this time from her seat in Parliament. The provocation was her opposition to TADA. Mamata put the Rao government in the dock for allowing the law—grossly misused against Muslims—to continue.[12] Not least among her motives was gaining the confidence of Muslims in West Bengal. Senior Congress leaders informed her of how embarrassing it was to have one of their own MPs staging a public dharna and campaigning against such important legislative measures. Mamata's response? On 25 May 1995, she resigned from the Lok Sabha. She said that she had to choose between her status as an MP and the ethical call of her conscience. Six months later, at the Lok Sabha Speaker's request to 'forget' the misunderstanding, Mamata rejoined Parliament.

It is a puzzling thing, of course, that a leader as fiercely ambitious as Mamata gambled on resignations as a political strategy. The electorate of West Bengal, though initially impressed by her spirit of sacrifice, her indifference to privilege and posts, eventually grew weary and cynical. The signs of disaffection were clear; her resignations now brought scoffs of disdain. The political mileage Mamata hoped for turned into political liability. Even today, many sympathizers of the Left Front use such past behaviour as examples of her lack of finesse, her lack of knowledge of the fine art of statecraft. These commentators for the most part tend to forget that these were exactly the charges levelled against the communists when they struggled to come to power in the state.

She may have been cured of her resignation fetish, though. Her colleagues say that Mamata has realized that the people of West Bengal did not approve of her quitting as railway minister during the NDA regime; perhaps this was why she did not repeat the move in her latest tenure as the UPA government's railway minister, even when the Opposition bayed for her blood following a succession of train accidents and sabotages.

The 1980s and 1990s were Mamata's decades of struggle, when she battled enemies within and outside her party. As she claimed more and more Opposition space in West Bengal politics, powerful Congress leaders in the state pitted themselves against her. 'I knew all the powerful Congress leaders of Bengal were ranked against me. Some of them had been in constant touch with the CPI-M,' she writes.[13] She believed that they worked towards defeating her in the 1989 elections. The war in

West Bengal Pradesh Congress Committee hit a high pitch on the issue of candidate selection for the 1996 Lok Sabha polls. Somen Mitra's rivals Priya Ranjan Dasmunshi and Subrata Mukherjee aligned with Mamata, who in turn backed Subrata's bid to lead the Congress Legislative Party. Running into severe opposition from Somen, Subrata Mukherjee dropped out of the fray. Mamata then decided to run a parallel state unit of the Congress, comprising Subrata's and her followers.

In the run-up to the 1996 polls, Mamata was at the centre of dramatic scenes unfolding on Kolkata's streets. Accusing the Congress of fielding incompetent, ineligible candidates, she refused to contest, provoking a hysterical outpouring from her followers. Amid high-pitched melodrama, Mamata yet again threatened to hang herself with her fabled black shawl. Her supporters drummed up delirious protests, encircling their leader, pleading, coaxing and crying. Their over-the-top display of affection worked. Mamata retracted her decision, filed her nomination and won from the South Kolkata constituency. This is how she got her third term in Parliament.

The 1996 general elections threw up a fractured mandate, bringing about new alignments and realignments of political forces. The formation of a Congress-backed United Front government, with the Left parties playing a crucial role in its formation and functioning was not good news for Mamata. In addition, Mamata continued to bear the brunt of the severe internecine warfare within the Congress state unit. In 1997, she fought the West Bengal Pradesh Congress Committee elections against Somen Mitra and lost by twenty-seven votes.

With her existence in the Congress becoming more and more uncomfortable, Mamata decided on a clean break.

Splitting the party, she formed her own outfit—the Trinamool (grass roots) Congress—in 1998. She could finally focus on an uncompromised, unbridled fight against the Left Front, unfettered by the new-found camaraderie between the Congress and the Left in Delhi. Indian politics seemed to be turning a corner as the CPI-M firmed up its support to the Congress, branding the BJP its main enemy, as new political challenges arose at the national level.

This messy backdrop to Mamata's emergence as a political protagonist is important in understanding her psyche and her definition of herself as a 'victim'—of the CPI-M and the Congress. The slippery politics of the Congress's West Bengal unit contributed in no small measure to Mamata's anxieties about conspiracies. Then, as leader of the Opposition, Mamata did not trust the Congress. As chief minister now, she continues to distrust them—a feeling the Congress returns in full measure.

Mamata's victory at this critical juncture of West Bengal politics belongs to her alone. Her party, now in power, has eventually come to represent the 'real' Congress. One by one, all of her former adversaries—former Congress bigwigs Somen Mitra, Subrata Mukherjee, Saugata Roy—have swallowed their pride and joined the Trinamool.

But even in 2011, the Trinamool and the Congress had a difficult time arriving at an electoral alliance. The conspiratorial network that had once worked overtime to pull Mamata down was weaker now, but still active. 'A Congress–CPI-M entente is still a reality. Ninety-nine per cent of Congress leaders and rank and file are against the Trinamool Congress,' Subrata Mukherjee told me. Trinamool leaders view Pranab Mukherjee, finance minister and second-in-command in the Delhi durbar, with a great deal of suspicion. 'He is close to the CPI-M. After all, let us not forget that at the age of seventy, he won the Jangipur seat with the CPI-M's help,' a senior Trinamool leader said.

Trinamool and the NDA Phase

Mamata chose 1 January 1998, coinciding with the Kalpataru festival held in memory of Ramakrishna Paramahansa, to announce the formation of the Trinamool Congress. Krishna Bose writes of that day, 'The Trinamool Congress was born at a historic function at the five-corner junction of Shyambazaar. It was born amid sweeping expectations of the people that a real alternative to the ruling party had emerged.'[14]

Before we proceed, a brief note on the backdrop against which Trinamool was born is required. The AICC was in session in Kolkata's Netaji Indoor Stadium in August 1997. By this time, relations between Mamata and the Congress's central leadership were acidic. Her followers had been deliberately kept out of the session. In protest, Mamata boycotted the 'indoor conclave' and, on 9 August, held her own session outdoors. Preparing the political and ideological ground for fracturing the Congress, Mamata cited as examples Subhash Chandra Bose and Indira Gandhi and the historical contexts in which they had formed their parties, the Forward Bloc and the Congress (I) respectively. '[…] why then should we not build a separate platform to awaken our leaders in Delhi from their slumber and strengthen our party? We therefore decided to conduct our fight from the platform of the Trinamool Congress from that day,' Mamata writes.[15] She invited Sonia Gandhi to the session. The Congress chief, of course, stayed away.

The indoor vs outdoor sessions were also emblematic of how Mamata perceived the two parties: the Congress was a party of dark conspiracies and undercover plots hatched inside closed doors, while the Trinamool Congress was a party of light and transparency, well equipped to fight the Left without being saddled with the compulsions of Delhi's realpolitik and West Bengal's factional strife. Mamata, however, did not make a formal announcement of the split. She still looked towards Sonia Gandhi to reverse the process. But the writing on the wall was clear.

As the United Front government collapsed and parliamentary elections approached, the Trinamool Congress committee demanded an active role in the selection of candidates. 'For a while, I have been urging Sonia Gandhi to take charge of the Congress party. The party cannot continue to function in this manner. Each time however she [Sonia Gandhi] turned down my request. Still I continued to rush to 10 Janpath because of my special regard for Rajiv Gandhi,' Mamata wrote at the time.[16] The situation was becoming untenable. Pranab Mukherjee's camaraderie with the Somen Mitra faction kept Mamata on tenterhooks and her conspiracy theories alive.

Sensing irreversible changes ahead, Sonia Gandhi summoned Mamata to Delhi. She urged Mamata to work within the Congress, and delegated to Oscar Fernandes the responsibility of taking into consideration Mamata's grievances and accommodating her candidates. According to Mamata, Fernandes disappeared without a word, leaving her in the dark. By then, she believed the delay to be a trap to deny the Trinamool Congress time to register itself with the Election Commission within the mandatory deadline. Mamata started drawing up the registration papers with help from Congress colleagues Pankaj Banerjee and Sudip

Bandyopadhyay. Meanwhile, the Congress high command tried to neutralize the bickering factions in West Bengal, negotiating deals on the one hand with Mamata Banerjee and on the other with Somen Mitra. Mamata was not wrong about the basic strategy of the Congress leadership: to buy time and to make sure she missed the Election Commission's registration deadline.

Not to be outwitted, she sent the registration papers clandestinely to the Election Commission. Faced with her stubbornness, the Congress leadership gave in. The high command agreed to replace the Congress Election Committee with a new Congress Electioneering Committee. Most importantly, Mamata was to head the committee. But the twists and turns did not end there. Even as the Congress leadership went public about Mamata's new post, AICC president Sitaram Kesri, at a press conference in Hyderabad, declared that Mamata had been appointed chairperson of the election's Publicity Committee. Furious, Mamata saw this as yet another Congress ploy to stab her in the back by misleading her with contradictory announcements. She decided to make the split formal. Mamata may well have already made up her mind to part ways with her parent party. Kesri's announcement was probably just the last straw.

This brings us to 1 January 1998 and the formal announcement of the formation of the Trinamool Congress from the Chittaranjan Park, New Delhi, residence of Ajit Panja, a senior member of the party and a former minister of state in the Central government. During the press conference, Mamata came to know of her six-year expulsion from the Congress.

The next phase of her career was spent in the company of the BJP and the NDA government, which raised disquieting questions about her secular credentials. Then prime minister Atal Bihari Vajpayee was the first, in fact, to appoint her railway minister. Did siding with the BJP-led NDA government—especially her continuing to support it even after the 2002 pogrom in Gujarat[17]—make Mamata an accomplice in a communal game plan? Did it dent her secular credentials?

Rather than seeing her support of the NDA in purely moral terms, it is more interesting to analyse the political dynamics that 'forced' her down a certain path, without compromising her potential to strike a political chord with voters at large. Mamata's dalliance with the NDA seemed to vindicate her unflinching commitment to a single-issue political agenda: removing the Left Front government from West Bengal. She moved within this narrow political grid, juggling her loyalties, leaning towards one bloc or the other, aligning with whichever party seemed to her the most aggressive in its willingness to fight the Left. Not secularism or communalism, neo-liberal or socialist, the only ideology Mamata stayed unwaveringly true to was an all-out combat against the CPI-M. It is important to note, again, that in this respect Mamata is closer to Mayawati than, say, Lalu Prasad, for whom secular political ideals always took precedence over electoral tactics.

Soon after the Trinamool Congress was formed, Mamata made it clear that she did not consider the BJP untouchable, leaving the door ajar for her to cross over to the other side. 'Since untouchability is an unparliamentary word in the tradition of parliamentary democracy, I am not ready to label any political party "untouchable"', she writes, defending her decision. 'Our fight against the CPI-M is essentially political. Though we have been fighting them for a long time, and though they have killed many of our workers and sympathizers, and unleashed terror, we have never used this label (untouchable) to define the CPI-M.'[18]

Krishna Bose says that, despite the 'huge ideological gap' between the BJP and the Trinamool Congress, the simple philosophy of 'my enemy's enemy is my friend', provided Mamata with enough of a justification to join forces with the BJP.

The 1998 Lok Sabha elections came early in the life of an infant Trinamool Congress. Though still unsteady on its feet, the fledgling party contested twenty-nine out of West Bengal's forty-two parliamentary constituencies, leaving thirteen seats to the BJP. The poll results were beyond the expectations of Mamata and her party. They bagged seven seats and a little over 24 per cent of the votes, greatly bolstering the party's morale. The BJP managed to win one seat. The Congress too won a single seat out of the thirty-nine it contested, and even that with a 15.2 per cent vote share, indicative of the dire straits the party was in. The Trinamool emerged from these elections looking like a viable political alternative.

And so began the next lap of Mamata Banerjee's journey: as a fellow traveller of the NDA, a formation directly in conflict with her parent party. Vajpayee invited Mamata to join his government, which she refused to do. Instead, the Trinamool Congress committed itself to lending outside support. Joining the government, Mamata argued, would compromise her party's autonomy. She must have been motivated also by her deep conviction that spurning privilege and rank goes down well with the people, fed up as they are of leaders chasing fancy designations and ministerial berths. Instead, she used her status as an important partner of the NDA to push forward her agenda in Bengal.

But Mamata continued to be restless. Plagued by uncertainties and dilemmas, she oscillated between putting in resignation letters and retracting them. The tag of 'unpredictability' she had picked up in the early years of her political life stuck even more firmly.

At the core tactical 'combat Left' level, the Trinamool Congress shared with the BJP a bond deeper than it did with the Congress. While the BJP's animus towards the Left was primarily ideological, to the Trinamool, it was simply a question of wresting power from the Marxists. As Mamata has often said, especially in the context of the 2011 assembly elections campaign, she does not necessarily have a problem with leftist ideology. Indeed, her party has been flooded by former Marxist-Leninists in the aftermath of the Singur and Nandigram agitations. Mamata has even charged the CPI-M with deviating from Marxist principles.

The BJP hoped that an alliance with Mamata would help it make inroads into West Bengal, where, despite the existence of a communal vote bank, the party had been unable to make electoral headway. Thanks to the Trinamool, for the first time in 1998, the BJP was able to open its electoral account in the state. Mamata, on her part, tried to extract her pound of flesh from the NDA. Taking up the plea of a law and order breakdown in West Bengal, from time to time, she pressured the government to bring the 'anarchic' state under President's Rule. But electorally, the 1998 elections did not help the Trinamool Congress improve its presence. In the panchayat elections of May 1998, it performed badly, even though many Congress workers deserted their sinking ship to board the Trinamool. Mamata was restive, belligerent; her alliance with the BJP had not been received well among Muslim supporters, especially in the urban pockets. Her party's dull performance in the local polls and the NDA government's obvious reluctance to dismiss the Left Front government made her increasingly peevish. Looking for a way to cut her losses, Mamata suspended her support to the NDA government and then retracted her decision when coaxed by L.K. Advani, second-in-command in the BJP and the NDA government.

The Trinamool got a break in 2000, even though it was accompanied by high political violence. The by-elections in Panskura in Medinipur district took place in June of that year, following the death of CPI MP Geeta Mukherjee, who had represented the constituency as many as seven times. The elections took place amid bloody clashes between the CPI-M and the Trinamool. The CPI candidate, Gurudas Das Gupta, was pitted against Trinamool Congress's Bikram Sarkar, a relatively fresh entrant into politics. Mamata tried to cobble together a mahajot—a grand alliance of the Trinamool Congress, BJP and the Congress—against the Left Front. The Congress put up a candidate even though the party's campaign on the ground was weak. The importance of this election was two fold: it triggered unprecedented violence in which large numbers of workers from both the CPI-M and the Trinamool Congress were hurt, and it saw the victory of Bikram Sarkar, signalling the retreat of the Left in one of its traditional pockets of strength. As violence escalated in Panskura, Mamata turned to the Central government once more, urging it to impose President's Rule in West Bengal.

Detecting an opportunity to put the Left Front government on the mat, the NDA government demanded an explanation from Chief Minister Jyoti Basu. The Congress demanded that West Bengal be declared a disturbed area. Teams from the Centre visited the violence-ravaged sites of Panskura. Inquiry missions were instituted. However, the suggestion that Article 356, President's Rule, be imposed met with a lukewarm response from the Centre and an outright rejection by regional parties like the DMK. Thwarted again, Mamata was unhappy with her tense alliance with the NDA, which was not yielding the political dividends she had hoped for.

But that year brought her an unexpected boost: Trinamool candidate Subrata Mukherjee defeated CPI-M's Kanti Ganguli, ending the Left's decade-long domination over the KMC. Buoyed by the results of the Panskura bypoll and the corporation elections, Mamata believed the positive trend would continue in the 2001 assembly elections. She was now worried that continued alliance with the BJP may damage her electoral prospects among Muslims, and so she prepared to sever her ties with the NDA. Following a hike by the Centre in petroleum prices, she sent her resignation to Vajpayee, with an ultimatum to roll back the hike in three days. Vajpayee, then undergoing a knee surgery in Mumbai, agreed in a written commitment to reconsider the matter once he was back in Delhi. Pacified, Mamata continued in the ministry.

But soon after, in 2001, Mamata once again put in her papers, this time following the news website *Tehelka*'s defence deals expose.[19] This time, Mamata made good on her threat and disengaged from the NDA. The only other Trinamool minister in the Vajpayee government, Ajit Panja, also quit the cabinet. The prodigal daughter aligned with the Congress and fought the West Bengal assembly elections jointly with the party she had so often labelled the CPI-M's 'B team'. After her party's victories in Panskura and the Kolkata Municipal Corporation, Mamata was confident about performing well in the assembly polls. She went into the campaign with the slogan 'Ebaar noi to never' (If not now, then never).

The poll outcome was a disaster. Trinamool's alliance with the Congress added just four seats to the tally of eighty-two that the undivided Congress had garnered. For the first time in over two decades, the CPI-M failed to gain a majority on its own, but its tally was down by only four seats compared to the last four assembly elections. A gutted Mamata locked herself in her room at her Kalighat residence.

'In 2001, the Trinamool Congress went through a tough time,' Krishna Bose confessed. Mamata attributed her poor electoral performance to rigging and submitted an eighteen-page memorandum to then president, K.R. Narayanan. Within her own party, trouble was simmering. Mamata had negotiated her alliance with the NDA impulsively, without political or administrative maturity. The people of West Bengal watched Mamata's unpredictable behaviour, at first bewildered, then exasperated and angry.

In the wake of the assembly results, serious differences cropped up between Mamata and senior Trinamool member Ajit Panja (who, you will remember, was forced to resign when Mamata did). The issue of contention: the party's relationship with the BJP and the NDA. Defiant, Panja opened a channel of communication with the BJP and lobbied for a cabinet berth. Retaliating, Mamata expelled him from the post of state unit president. But there was speculation about Mamata returning to the NDA after her party's dismal poll performance. She began negotiating with the BJP, which set out its own terms for renewing the partnership. Sensing that her resignation as railway minister had done little to enhance her popularity (and in fact diminished it), Mamata wanted the ministry back. The BJP refused to remove NDA's then railway minister, Nitish Kumar. Mamata was made to wait for over a year before she could rejoin the NDA in 2002—after then defence minister and NDA convener George Fernandes addressed a Trinamool Congress rally in Kolkata.

That was also the year that the genocide of Muslims in Gujarat cast a shadow over Chief Minister Narendra Modi and the NDA government at the Centre. The Trinamool was faced with a new dilemma. The NDA government was facing a no-confidence motion in Parliament. 'I had gone to Gujarat and seen with my own eyes what had happened. I was utterly shocked and believed we should vote against the NDA government in the Lok Sabha debate,' Krishna Bose told me. But she was in a minority when she expressed her opinion at a meeting of the Trinamool's Parliamentary Party, which finally voted in favour of the NDA.

In her book *Anubhuti*, Mamata tries to clear the air on the Gujarat issue. She writes about how she had petitioned Vajpayee to remove Narendra Modi from chief ministership and hand over charge to a person who would inspire the confidence of all sections of the people: '[…] we voted in favour of the government in the debate under Section 184, since the motion was specifically against the Central government. Despite the disquiet in our hearts, we voted in support, criticizing the Gujarat episode, if only in the interest of the government's stability.'[20] Her relationship with the NDA continued to be uneasy.

Mamata contextualized the conflict with the NDA within an ideological framework. She explained that the reasons for her conflict with the NDA should be understood in terms of a 'big' party (the BJP) moving away from the common agenda, which constituted the basis on which partners had joined the alliance. Attempting to counter her 'fickle, unstable ally' image, Mamata sought to put the onus on the BJP. She explained that religious controversies had been deliberately kept out of the NDA's common agenda at the time of its formation. But once the NDA government was in a stable position, a section within the BJP began to assert the core Hindutva agenda that had long been a central political programme of the BJP. Mamata specifically mentioned the raking up of the sensitive Ram temple issue. She took a dig at some NDA allies who, in their pursuit of ministerial posts and privilege, allowed themselves to be bullied by the 'Big Brother' in the alliance.

Throughout her political career, Mamata strived to construct and maintain a clean image: the eternal martyr, a leader nonchalantly turning her back on ministerial posts, scrupulously clean where matters of money were concerned in a political environment riddled with corruption. She mercilessly punished senior Trinamool leaders Ajit Panja and later Sudip Bandyopadhyay—who had both stood by her through her most turbulent years of political wilderness—because she believed they were manoeuvring for ministerial berths in the NDA cabinet. Clearly, she intended to portray herself and her party as symbols of selflessness, setting an example in matters of political altruism.

'Even today, she is given to pulling up Trinamool Congress ministers. A senior minister in the UPA was told point-blank by Mamata that she would strip him of his rank if he ignored calls from the public,' a Trinamool leader confided during an interview. Similarly, Mamata threatened to clip the wings of an MP who she believed was desperately keen to head the railway ministry after the Trinamool won the assembly elections and it was clear Mamata would move back to the state.

It is worth mentioning though, that notwithstanding her protestations that rank and privilege matter little to her, Mamata did not hesitate to campaign against her successor in the railway ministry, Nitish Kumar, when she wanted the post back.

The year or so that Mamata was out in the cold before she rejoined the NDA in August 2002 was a particularly difficult phase for her. 'The Trinamool will take revenge for the way the party has been humiliated on its home turf of Bengal. No power can stall us in our path of progress. I can only "feel" for those who believe this to be an epitaph of the Trinamool. Wait till the bugle of war is heard again. We have not been born to lose. We will return to the homes of the ordinary people. It is just a matter of time,' she wrote around that time.[21] In September 2003, Mamata re-entered the NDA cabinet as a minister without portfolio. Three months later, she was appointed Union minister of coal and mines—ironically, a fortnight before the Lok Sabha was dissolved.

But even in that short period, Mamata made a string of announcements. Within forty-eight hours of assuming office, she declared a 15 per cent wage revision for over a lakh of mine workers, when the trade unions' demand was only for a 12.5 per cent revision. She also withdrew a Bureau of Industrial and Financial Reconstruction package, which had recommended closure of sixty-four mines. In her characteristic style, Mamata declared that not a single mine would be shut down, throwing a spanner in the Left's agitations against the closure of mines.

But Mamata seemed to have lost the plot. Her party was just not picking up in West Bengal, and the CPI-M, despite burgeoning discontent on the ground, seemed to hold its own. In the 2004 general elections, the Trinamool crashed to an all-time low, winning only a solitary seat—that of its president Mamata Banerjee. At the Centre, the Congress soundly defeated the BJP-led NDA and headed a coalition that remained crucially dependent on the Left parties for its survival. The performance of the Left far exceeded all its previous records. With sixty-three MPs, they formed their largest ever contingent in Parliament. The Trinamool continued to be in an alliance with the BJP from 2004 until the agitation in Singur erupted in 2006.

Prior to that historic moment in the Trinamool's transition, Mamata Banerjee's party had become a political washout—a toothless contender against the Left. In fact, even diehard optimists and blind party loyalists would not have anticipated such a drastic turnabout. In 2005, the Trinamool lost the prestigious Kolkata Municipal Corporation to the Left. A resurgent Left Front seemed more in charge than before, both at the Centre and in the state. The Congress was, once again, working in sync with Mamata's sworn enemy, the CPI-M.

Breaking Out on Her Own

Mamata wasn't one to stay down. She kept up her party's protests on the street. Meanwhile, the new chief minister, Buddhadeb Bhattacharjee, dazzled by his own and his party's success, confidently stepped up his industrialization drive. On 20 October 2005, Mamata and her party workers stood soaking in the rain outside the Taj Hotel, protesting the government's decision to hand over farmland in Howrah to the Indonesia-based Salim Group of industries. At that time, they could not have known that that protest was the beginning of a turn in their fortunes.

In the 2006 assembly elections, the Left Front had managed to increase its tally of seats from 199 to 235, and return confident and victorious to Writers' Buildings. With just thirty seats, the Trinamool Congress seemed to be a spent force that was in no position to challenge the Left Front's supremacy. But, as the Left embarked on an undemocratic land acquisition drive, grumbles of discontent could clearly be heard. Neither the CPI-M nor the Trinamool could have foreseen the political storm awaiting them—a storm that would blow one away and bring in the other.

The Road to Writers' Buildings

The fast-paced events between 2006 and 2008 revealed the deep fault lines in the Left Front's base. The CPI-M was virtually coming apart at the seams. In 2008, the Trinamool won the panchayat polls. The next year, it gained further momentum during the Lok Sabha polls. The tide had begun to turn.

Unbelievable as it sounds, the seemingly invincible Left was brought down through peasant struggles. The agitation against land acquisition for industry in Nandigram and Singur, tribal upsurge against police atrocities, and decades of misgovernance in Lalgarh formed the backdrop for the Trinamool Congress's overwhelming success. In Delhi, the Indo-US Nuclear Deal axed Left–Congress conviviality and led to the former's withdrawal of support to the Manmohan Singh government. The path for a mahajot was now clear. But by the end of the Nandigram–Singur resistance movement, Mamata seemed capable of going the whole distance alone. And the 'B team of the CPI-M' needed the Trinamool to keep the party's masthead above water.

The 2009 Lok Sabha election results were Mamata's moment of glory. The Left Front went down from sixty-odd seats to fifteen. The only person from the Trinamool to have won a seat in the last parliamentary elections, in 2004, an ecstatic Mamata now saw her party not only recover its losses but even make a profit. The Trinamool won nineteen seats. The Opposition alliance won eleven seats more than the Left—the Congress won six and the SUCI one. The remaining seat went to the BJP. The Trinamool was on a roll. The humiliation and frustration of years of failure retreated in the face of the party's seemingly unstoppable march to power. In 2010, Mamata's party won twenty-seven of the eighty-one civic bodies, including the Kolkata Municipal Corporation and the neighbouring Bidhannagar Municipality. This sensational result was particularly sweet for Mamata, coming as it did after her differences with the Congress over seat-sharing in the municipal polls. Eventually, the allies went their separate ways. The predictions were that, with its alliance with the Congress having come undone, the Trinamool would suffer a setback.

For years Mamata had smarted under insults: Congress leaders trampling all over her, denying her a place in the sun. The formation of the Trinamool was the first step on the road to projecting her party as the 'real' Congress. Thirteen long years of a roller-coaster ride later, the victories from 2008 to 2010 were Mamata's vindication. The Left parties could win only eighteen municipalities, as against forty-nine in the 2005 elections, while the Congress won seven as against twelve in 2005. The Left also lost the Bidhannagar Municipality, which it had held for three consecutive terms. The Trinamool Congress secured ninety-five of the 141 wards of the Kolkata Municipal Corporation. The Left

Front won merely thirty-three wards, forty-two less than before; even the Congress's tally halved from twenty to ten. The Congress must have secretly rued the Trinamool Congress romping home on its own strength, robbing the junior partner of any clout it may have hoped to have. A 'semi-final' is how Mamata described the municipal election results. It was with this historic victory setting a precedent that the Trinamool Congress would go into the 'finals'—the assembly polls in 2011—she said.

Eventually, after much dithering and several hiccups, the alliance between the Trinamool Congress and the Congress firmed up in the 2011 assembly elections, sealing the fate of the tottering Left Front government, and bringing Mamata Banerjee to power.

The thirteen-year-old Trinamool Congress has now entered the adult phase of its life. This raises several questions about how it has fared as a political party since its birth as a splinter group of the Congress, and its recent reincarnation as the 'real' Congress? 'The Congress (mainstream) will exist if it keeps its association with the Trinamool Congress. By moving away from the latter, the Congress will only marginalize itself further,' Saugata Roy said to me as the elections approached.

But after more than a decade in politics, what kind of a party structure does the Trinamool Congress have? What is its programmatic vision, apart from the core objective of removing the Left Front government from power? Will it be able to reinvent itself as a 'responsible' party in its changed role?

The Trinamool Congress is essentially an inchoate body with an all-powerful deity in the form of Mamata Banerjee presiding over it. Many among Mamata's colleagues describe the party as a fan club, and argue that its members are bound by their shared admiration, awe and even terror of its president. The Trinamool does not have an organizational structure. The core committees exist only on paper. Sudip Bandyopadhyay, however, maintains that a party organization, though absent earlier, is now very much in place and functioning. 'The core committees now meet at least once in a month,' he told me. But a majority tend to agree that Mamata Banerjee is the party.

Some political observers offer an inverted rationalization for the dishevelled structure of the Trinamool: that a flexible, non-hierarchical party is a 'historical necessity' at this juncture of West Bengal politics. Others maintain that the non-structured character of the Trinamool was by deliberate design. A senior Trinamool Congress leader claimed that Mamata Banerjee realized early on that her party was ill-equipped to take on the CPI-M's mighty organizational structure, with its complex network, which transacts day-to-day business and politics in the state and has been doing so for over three decades. 'She realized that removing the CPI-M by building a competitive organizational structure was not possible. Call it her thinking or strategy, what Mamata Banerjee aimed at was building a people's movement that would make the Trinamool Congress a force to reckon with,' he explained.

Luckily for Mamata, the Left Front government embarked on its disastrous expedition of violent land acquisition in Singur and Nandigram in 2006. Mamata's thesis that a people's uprising would finally change political equations worked wonders. Even with an amorphous party organization, without any ideological moorings, the Trinamool hollowed out the ground on which the CPI-M had stood so arrogantly strong. The mighty organization bit the dust, while a virtually formless Trinamool suddenly found its feet.

But until the Singur and Nandigram protests, the Trinamool had no compact social or political base. It was primarily regarded as a party with a following among the urban youth, street hawkers, slum dwellers, illegal settlers and workers in the informal sector. And, of course, the sections that were against the Left Front government. Till 2006, despite being at the receiving end of widespread resentment and anger, the CPI-M continued to be regarded as the party of the poor. The Trinamool, on the other hand, was considered a party of the landed gentry in the villages. But that was before Singur and Nandigram shifted, virtually overnight, the course of West Bengal politics. None of this is to suggest that Singur and Nandigram were unique starting points of discontent. But both—especially the latter—on the one hand showed the masses of Bengal that it was possible to challenge the might of the Left Front, and on the other, brought to the forefront a whole range of administrative malaises that had plagued the state for decades. The question of land and livelihood in Singur and Nandigram brought the development agenda to the forefront of politics in West Bengal.

A comparison of the CPI-M's and the Trinamool's organizational structures is an exercise in pointlessness because of the uneven terrains on which they are located. Mamata Banerjee's party is in no position, theoretically or practically, to emulate the centralized, hierarchical organizational structure of the CPI-M. It may not even aspire to such a structure. But ironically, the Trinamool, too, is a centralized party, the difference being that all power is invested in one single individual: Mamata Banerjee. She embodies the hierarchy and the control; from her alone come the fiats, the reprimands, and the occasional praise. Briefly put, Mamata Banerjee is the sum and substance of the party she leads.

The issue of organizational structure has been rearing its head frequently over the past few years. During the Lalgarh movement, and its subsequent takeover by the Maoists, two distinct visions of democracy and organizations were seen—one decentralized and spontaneous, the other hierarchical, rigid and disciplined. For those on the Left of the political spectrum who opposed Mamata, but did want an alternative to the ruling Left Front, her one-person style reeks of political problems. They look for other modes of politics, of organizing resistance. At the same time, given that Mamata Banerjee has skilfully placed herself at the very centre of the movement for change in Bengal, one wonders whether such judgements are not too hasty. Some people I spoke to suggested that only a rigid, one-person, top-down, semi-authoritarian style of politics could challenge the organizational might of the Left Front. You needed a centre of gravity around which the political opposition could crystallize. This is what seems to have happened with Mamata, and this is what has brought her where she is today.

3

The Making of Mamata Banerjee

On 16 August 1990, through the perverse logic of violence, Mamata entered a new phase of her political career. Even ahead of the dastardly assault at Hazra junction that day, which left her hanging on to life by a frayed thread, there were signs that she was in imminent danger. The Kolkata Police was trailing the Congress activist on a 24x7 surveillance duty, presumably relaying her activities and movements, whom she was speaking with, and so on to the higher-ups.

The police surveillance, Rajiv Gandhi's warning and reports from colleagues and friends had all created an atmosphere of dark foreboding. 'My mother was scared. She was constantly telling me the night before, "You must not go out. They will finish you." I had lied when I had reassured her that I would not go out. I had issued a call for the procession and my not turning up would be nothing but my defeat,'[1] writes Mamata.

And so, Mamata stepped out of her Kalighat residence and walked towards Hazra junction as part of the procession. On reaching the crossroad, she saw a group armed with guns, iron rods and stout wooden sticks advance threateningly towards her. Among the eyewitnesses was Kalyan Banerjee, an advocate, now a Trinamool Congress MP, who was on his way to Hazra. Sniffing trouble ahead, he took shelter in a shop. From that safe vantage point, he witnessed the savagery of the attack. In a swift, military-like operation, the assailants, brandishing their weapons, cleared the area and took charge, ensuring that bystanders did not rush to the target's rescue.

Mamata's colleagues dragged her to a Bata storefront opposite the Radhakrishna temple at Hazra. But the attackers had come prepared. Swinging his stick, Laloo Alam, a CPI-M worker, hit Mamata hard on the head, she writes in her memoirs. 'The right side of my head (just a hairline away from where the brain is) had cracked open and I was bleeding profusely. I was still undeterred. I was trying to see what their goal was. When I saw them getting ready to hit me on the head with an iron rod, strangely, in that grave circumstance, I covered my head with my hands,' Mamata narrates.[2] That instinctive gesture was, according to her, a stroke of divine intervention.

The blow crushed her wrist. Mamata blacked out. She regained consciousness in Alipore's Woodlands Nursing Home. Over the next few days, Mamata battled death tooth-and-nail like she would the CPI-M, her most intimate adversary. The doctors weren't sure they could save her. People say she dodged death by a mere whisker.

Recalling the events of that day, Saugata Roy says: 'I was an MLA back then. At the hour of attack I was not present at the site. Later I went to PG Hospital where Mamata Banerjee's wounds were being dressed.' In a critical condition, she was shifted to the Woodlands Nursing Home.

The news of the horrific attack and Mamata's critical injuries spread like wildfire through Kolkata. 'At the nursing home, people would queue up to see her as though she were a deity at a place of worship. Congress workers had to manage the steady stream of people who kept coming,' says Prabir Ghosal, then a reporter with *Bartaman Patrika*.

A story in journalistic circles goes somewhat like this: *Bartaman Patrika* editor Barun Sengupta, a diehard supporter of Mamata since her days of political anonymity, was going to write his column at a time when it didn't look like she would survive. Kolkata was agog with rumours and speculation. Top CPI-M leaders, it is said, called up Sengupta, requesting him not to let out the fact that Mamata was teetering on the cusp of life and death. They said that the information, given the volatile public mood, could trigger a riot. Could the CPI-M be so arrogant as to underrate the impact this would have on the public mood? But then again, even Mamata's own colleagues in the Congress were taken aback by the serpentine queues outside the hospital.

The 16 August attack was a grisly marker, a sinister portent of more onslaughts to come. It also created around the Congress leader an aura of victimhood, suddenly scaling her image up several notches. CPI-M, on the other hand, found itself completely discredited. The question everyone asked was: how could the ruling party have stooped so low as to attempt to murder one of its most aggressive combatants in broad daylight at a busy crossroad in the heart of south Kolkata? The incident also showed Mamata up as an activist—flawed, hot-headed and impulsive to a fault—but not wanting in courage. This gave Mamata her second 'break' in politics after her spectacular victory from the Jadavpur constituency in the 1984 Lok Sabha elections.

But even before the Hazra Road attack, Mamata's abundant courage, sheer energy and her militant, if rowdy, protests had drawn the attention of Congress leaders, particularly Rajiv Gandhi. He had been trying for a while to appoint Mamata president of the Youth Congress. Much to his frustration, Mamata's detractors in the Congress—of which there were a fair few—would derail the proposal each time. The West Bengal unit of the Congress was a snake pit of back-room manipulations and conspiracies, with its various factions trying to do each other in. Rajiv's opportunity came when Mamata was critical and under medical supervision at the Woodlands Nursing Home. This time, he virtually rammed Mamata's appointment through. Mamata heard of this keenly awaited appointment as she was lying on the nursing home bed. In her autobiography, she mentions that Rajiv bore the entire cost of her medical treatment. He even wanted to send her for recuperation to the United States.

The Hazra Road incident was a precursor to yet another horrifying attack on Congress activists on 21 July 1993. On that day, CPI-M cadres and the state police ran amok on the streets of Kolkata, savaging Youth Congress members who, led by their president, were laying siege to Writers' Buildings. Thirteen of them were killed in random firing. The Esplanade area morphed into a war zone. Tear gas shells were burst, shots were fired, lathis were wielded to injure or kill. Mamata was assaulted and had to be admitted to hospital, unconscious, a second time.

Since then, the Congress and later the Trinamool Congress have been observing Shahid Divas every 21 July through rallies and public meetings. Before 2010, however, the observance of this day was just a dry ritual. But the Shahid Divas of 2010, coming in the wake of the Trinamool Congress's electoral victories from the panchayat to the parliamentary level, was unlike any other. The mood was upbeat, even as the ground was being prepared for the assembly elections.

'The 21 Julys that followed the fateful day till last year were but a political showdown that failed to inspire much confidence among the participants about their goal ever becoming fulfilled. But today they came not only to show their strength to the CPI-M, but also to display their supreme conviction that the end of the Marxist regime is but a formality and only a few months away. Mr Brindaban Das and his wife Malati Das who came from Vrindaban epitomized the mood when they said: "We used to come every year when we were in Balurghat in South Dinajpur. This year we came a day earlier. For, we were aware this year there will be a record turnout to prepare for the change. We are sure Didi will come to power and we will have our own government soon,"' wrote Uday Basu in a report for the *Statesman*.[3]

To understand the background to the 21 July attack, we need to rewind a few months to 25 November 1992, when Mamata staged a show of strength at the sprawling Brigade Parade Ground. The huge gathering was intended to relay a message—a warning to the ruling party that the Trinamool Congress was going to press through, regardless of threats, assaults and abuses. The many attacks on Mamata were obviously connected to the ruling Left Front government's increasing discomfort with the political opposition becoming powerful, posing a threat.

By 2010, however, Mamata Banerjee had become too dominant a personality and presence in Bengal politics to be 'removed' in the violent ways attempted during the 1990s. As the ferocity of the physical attacks ebbed and the CPI-M and its allies adopted other means of discrediting her politics and persona, cultural factors became important. One of the most significant of these—as made clear in the recent past by the sexist comments of former CPI-M MP Anil Basu—was the legacy of gender and sexual politics in West Bengal.

A Woman Among Men

To understand how Mamata Banerjee, without the backing of a political luminary, a male relative, partner or benefactor, created her own space in politics, it is important to stop and consider gender and Left politics in West Bengal. Equally relevant is the presence of a strong misogynist element in Bengali culture, even as it claims to revere women. (Watch Satyajit Ray's *Devi* for a potent examination of this.) Reverential it may be, but only with regard to women who conform to a traditional image. Every political party here has tended to project women leaders who have a 'good, maternal, bhadra' image. With her single-woman status, her loud mouth and her abrasive, forthright style, Mamata embodies the contrarian woman—threatening to the genteel bhadralok sensibility. The possibility that the Trinamool Congress may ascend to power—that they may be ruled by 'a woman like Mamata'—was, not so long back, a 'nightmare' for many in West Bengal.

The politics of womanhood in Bengal is deeply connected to the massive culture of violence. According to Raka Ray, who researched women's movements and politics in Bengal, the CPI-M's women's wing, Paschim Banga Ganatantrik Mahila Samiti (PBGMS) had cited 'political reasons' to be behind the 'most violent and vindictive forms' of rape. 'A former CPI-M member of Parliament views rape and other forms of sexual assault and harassment as stemming from criminals usually associated with the Congress Party.'[4] During the thirty-four years of Left Front rule, party cadres, aided and abetted by the police, used rape as an instrument to exercise political control. The ruling CPI-M's refusal to book party leaders and cadres implicated in these cases legitimized the use of violence against women.

In the land of the Marxist bhadralok who consider themselves rightful heirs to the Bengal Renaissance, ostensibly the torchbearers of enlightened attitude towards women, Mamata was vulnerable because of her gender, when she was a young activist and, later, even as leader of the Opposition. The CPI-M leveraged gender as a weapon to trivialize, even vulgarize, their rhetoric of attack on the Trinamool Congress president, her status as a single woman without the bulwark of exotic lineage or formidable rank of wealth and class shielding her.

In the aftermath of clashes with the police at Singur, Mamata complained of having been hurt in the chest. At a subsequent press conference, a top CPI-M leader told the media, 'Onar eto buke kano lage boloon to?' (Why does she get hurt on her chest so much?).[5] Another time, a senior party leader threatened to drag the Opposition leader by her hair to her Kalighat residence. More recently, a former CPI-M MP and a prominent party leader asked at a public meeting how a slogan like Maa, Maati, Manush could be coined by Mamata Banerjee, who was not herself a mother. There was a time when CPI-M leaders at meetings and rallies asked parents not to name their daughters 'Mamata'. They sniggered about film actor and MP Shatabdi Roy, tittering that the Trinamool Congress had fielded 'street women' who wear make-up. Further back, in 2007, senior party leader Benoy Konar called upon CPI-M cadres in Nandigram to bare their buttocks to Medha Patkar and Mamata if they dared enter the area. A CPI-M leader was heard saying that Mamata should be whacked on her buttocks. That these were not just vile utterances of individuals is borne out by the fact that not a single leader of the CPI-M, male or female, either in A.K. Gopalan Bhavan, the CPI-M's national headquarters or Alimuddin Street, the state headquarters, censured those making these comments. If anything, the gleeful backslapping and disdainful laughter that followed showed tacit endorsement of what would be, in an office environment, a clear case of sexual harassment.

On her part, Mamata treated the volley of indignities with utter disdain. But the sheer 'physicality' of the CPI-M's opposition can be gauged from the assaults and indignities Mamata suffered at the hands of its cadres and the state police, which was at the beck and call of Alimuddin Street, the CPI-M's headquarters. Particularly alarming was the way the senior comrades set an example, using a stridently masculine tenor to humiliate Mamata. The sheer unrelenting nature of the abuse granted legitimacy to a political rhetoric of crudeness, sexism and violence.

The space of a democratic discourse between the ruling party and its Opposition was taken up largely by the brutal exercise of majority power. The slogans raised by those attending the CPI-M's public meeting at the Brigade Parade Ground in February 2011, just a few months ahead of the assembly elections, were a further indication of the many ways in which the party leadership had encouraged the cadres to pull no punches. 'Kalighater mynah shilpa hote dai na' (This mynah from Kalighat does not allow industry to come up); 'Didi theke didima mukhyamantri hobe na' (From elder sister to grandmother, you will never become chief minister). In both slogans, Mamata is targeted as woman. 'Kalighater mynah'—a slight that makes her out to be capricious, trivial and talkative like the mynah bird, lacking the intellectual capacity to realize the serious implications of stalling industrialization in Bengal. Incidentally, the mynah slight is reserved exclusively for women. The second slogan carries disparaging references to Mamata's age; in a state where most politicians of Mamata's status are decades older than her, it's telling that the digs should be directed at her age. The onus of youth, after all, rests solely on women.

As Mamata looked set to become West Bengal's first woman chief minister—and maybe even the architect of a turnabout in the state, initiating a new political culture—the talk in CPI-M circles got increasingly morbid. In private banter, at public meetings, the party did not let go of a single opportunity to caricature Mamata as a *woman* driven by her mindless emotions, someone who needed tutoring in manners, etiquette and, of course, politics. Salacious jokes about her personal life or the perceived lack of it have been bandied about by senior CPI-M MPs in the corridors of Parliament. A strain of privilege emanating from masculinity, class, language and intellect underpinned the CPI-M's stream of abuses.

The unabashed attacks on Mamata's person and the string of verbal abuses are hardly a matter of surprise once contextualized in the overall culture of the party and the way communist parties the world over generally negotiate gender issues.

It is worth noting that Mamata, like many other women politicians, refuses to identify herself as a feminist. And the CPI-M, its incessant exhortations of women's rights notwithstanding, has unfailingly prioritized its partisan interests over everything else. The leaders have blithely looked the other way as long as the rapes, molestations and violence against their adversaries served the party's interests. Gender is a mere casualty in this war of attrition. The PBGMS, the CPI-M's nearly two-million-strong women's organization, with its elaborate hierarchical set-up, has fared disastrously as a women's organization, preferring to remain a handmaiden to it's male-dominated party. The members of the CPI-M's women's organization, rather than breaking conventional gender stereotypes, affirmed them in their lifestyles and dress code. 'The vast majority of the women I interviewed in the PBGMS were married and nearly half of them lived in joint families. More than 60 per cent did paid work outside the home—employed mainly as schoolteachers or full-time party workers,' observes Raka Ray.[6]

Nowhere does the Left's myth that it has breached the citadel of patriarchy and humanized gender relations stand more exposed than in the state they have ruled for thirty-four years. According to the West Bengal Crime Records Bureau, crimes against women have been on the rise.

Despite its pro-gender rhetoric in Delhi and West Bengal, the Left Front government failed to bring about qualitative changes in the lives of women in terms of health, education or attitudes to marital and sexual relations. In fact, the culture it promoted in the state further fortified the dominant elements of patriarchy. In addition, the CPI-M's unique electoral history elevated it to a near invincible position, where, without fear or apprehension, it could drive under the carpet every act of violence committed by its cadres. Starting with the Birati and Bantala cases of lynching, rape and murder, to Tapasi Malik from Singur—a teenager agitating against allocation of agricultural land to industry there—the party has left no stone unturned to shield the rapists and murderers in its ranks.

Within a few months of each other two horrifying incidents of violence, both implicating CPI-M workers, jolted West Bengal. In 1990, three women social workers were sexually assaulted—among them Anita Dewan was murdered in Bantala. On the heels of this incident three Bangladeshi women were raped in Birati. First, as a tempestuous agitator in the Congress, then as president of the Trinamool Congress, Mamata was always in the CPI-M's ballistic line of attack, a target of their chauvinistic, sexist abuse, their politics of violence. Not just her; the women of Singur and Nandigram bore on their bodies the full brunt of their assaults; almost as if the party had mandated brutality against the dissenters, even women.

Before trying to unravel Mamata's own understanding of gender and her relationship with feminism, if that does at all exist, I will fleetingly frame the CPI-M's negotiation of gender issues within the wider framework of the communist parties' gender code. A belief they hold dear is that women's employment is a precondition for their liberation from bondage. The implicit understanding is that economic liberation and class struggle, as well as participation in democratic movements, will automatically break the back of patriarchy. The language of women's empowerment used by communist leaders has often been grounded in traditional gender norms. In socialist countries, the 'right to work' has led to high employment among women. But as feminist and Marxist critic Frigga Haug points out, 'nowhere did women achieve decision-making positions in numbers that could sway masculinist cultures'.[7]

If the ruling communists in West Bengal turned the very notion of gendered politics on its head, in Kerala too, despite its strong Left presence, there is little to boast about. However, unlike West Bengal, the Left parties in Kerala shared power with the Congress, the electoral process ensuring neither remained at the helm of the state for more than five years. The communist and Congress codes on gender have been much the same. Women leaders of both political parties have been expected to conform to a stereotypical Indian image of 'ideal womanhood', especially in their attire and in their marital and sexual relations. In the assembly elections of 2011, Sindhu Joy, Kerala's first woman president of the CPI-M's student organization, quit the party, accusing it of 'pretensions on gender justice and issues of faith'. Joining the Congress, she said, 'How can the Chief Minister, Mr V.S. Achuthanandan, who cannot ensure fair treatment of women in the party, take care of [the] interests of women outside the party?'[8] The debased and chauvinistic quality of the attacks on Mamata have their roots in the general culture of communist parties, which, as it turns out, is not so radically different from others in the political class.

I come now to the crucial issues of Mamata's own engagement with gender and her understanding of her own identity as a woman. While she is that rarity, a self-made female leader, Mamata vehemently denies any affinity to feminism. 'She is not a feminist. Mamata is just Mamata,' writer Mahasweta Devi told me. Director Arpita Ghosh believes that even though Mamata may deny any connection to feminism, she has indeed 'lived her life as a feminist'. She had no benevolent male patron (except, for a very brief stint, Rajiv Gandhi), no father, brother, husband, partner prodding from the sidelines. The most special person in her life today is her mother. Despite many references in her books to members of her large family—sisters-in-law, brothers, nieces, nephews—the Trinamool president believes that her party is her 'very own family'. 'Politics and family are two distinct realms. In my life I consider the party and the grass-roots people as my very own family. The Trinamool Congress to me has become the Trinamool family; the reason why I feel so much...pain and anguish when an activist of the party is killed.'[9]

In the early years of her political career Mamata did have a tutor and a counsellor in Rajiv Gandhi. The brief stint of protective custodianship abruptly ended with Rajiv's death. But even when Rajiv Gandhi was alive, Mamata found herself in the company of Congressmen liaising with senior party leaders in Delhi, plotting to sabotage her career, to crash her soaring political ambitions to the ground. In the void following Rajiv's death, Mamata was left to defend herself against plots and counter-plots, often real, sometimes imaginary, hatched by her own party leaders to pull her down.

Though some may want to perceive in Rajiv Gandhi the role of Mamata's benefactor in the usual manner of Indian politics—as someone decisively contributing to her rise to fame—the argument does seem like a stretch. Rajiv was killed in 1991, long before Mamata's arrival as a leader to be truly reckoned with. Moreover, as I have pointed out earlier, despite his support of Mamata, Rajiv could not effectively neutralize the animosity of the state Congress leaders.

In fact, viewed through the gender lens, Mamata's story does indeed stand apart from the narratives of India's most powerful contemporary women leaders. Says Krishna Bose, 'Mamata has not been the widow, wife, daughter or companion of somebody.' Just to pick the three top women leaders in Indian politics today—Sonia Gandhi, Mayawati, J. Jayalalithaa—each has had a prop, a male guardian of compelling power, or a lineage of redoubtable political worth. The pull of the Nehru dynasty, the Congress's supreme mascot, dragged Rajiv's widow out of her cocooned, private existence, setting her on the path to becoming the most powerful person in Indian politics. But for the untimely death of her husband, Sonia was not likely to have strayed into the hurly-burly of politics and its messy transactions. Jayalalithaa, Tamil Nadu's formidable woman politician, a shrewd strategist, owed her political rise to M.G. Ramachandran (MGR), the iconic actor of the silver screen with whom she shared a personal relationship as well. Unlike the chaste and conventional Mamata, maintaining a safe distance from romance and love, Jayalalithaa lived as she willed, risking social disapproval and weathering nasty attacks from her political opponents. The actress-turned-politician collected photographs of Rock Hudson and admitted to being infatuated with cricketers like Nari Contractor and Mansur Ali Khan Pataudi. In the same trajectory as Jayalalithaa, Dalit leader Mayawati had Kanshi Ram introduce her to the arena of active politics. She also shared an intimate relationship with him.

Sujato Bhadra, of the Association for Protection of Democratic Rights (APDR), says Mamata, like Medha Patkar, the mass leader of the Narmada Bachao Andolan, does not challenge social and cultural conventions—or even the ground rules of patriarchy—through her politics or movements. 'I have worked with Medha Patkar. The one time I was living with some activists in Badwani, I saw a woman activist who was actively engaged with the movement, but still continued with the feudal practices in her family.' According to him, Medha believed in enlisting the support of the whole family and, therefore, did not risk their hostility by questioning the patriarchal, feudal norms.

In her books, Mamata deals with women's issues like gender-based violence, oppression, economic independence, and so on. As a minister in the Narasimha Rao government, she was briefly in charge of the Department of Women and Children. Her negotiation with gender is conventional and non-radical. In keeping with abstract principles of universal goodness and equality that she holds true, her understanding of women's issues is unmediated by complexities. She falls prey to nuggets of conventional 'wisdom'. For instance, she writes: 'We often find opportunist women from the upper social strata living as they want to. In the name of liberation, they greatly abuse their independence. If such a woman's family raises objections, she tends to use the law as a weapon of blackmail. Like many women, men too are victims of abuse.'[10] In another instance, she explains that women play a critical role in building a happy family and, therefore, contributing to the well-being of the society, but they are unfortunately also sometimes responsible for creating unrest in a family. Women often cannot stand other women, resulting in the mutual harassment of daughters-in-law and mothers-in-law. Undoubtedly, these are not the thoughts of a feminist.

The issue of domestic violence surfaces repeatedly in Mamata's books. Characteristically, she relates to these subjects through isolated incidents, personal experiences of the women she knew, her colleagues whose lives ended tragically. In her book *Ekante*, she narrates the experiences of three victims, Jharna, Anjali and Manju, two of whom took their own lives, while the third was set ablaze by her husband. Mamata's narrative does not indicate any effort on her part to contextualize domestic violence within the larger and pervasive phenomenon of patriarchy, control and masculine power. Perhaps this is not surprising given her proclivity to limit the scope of any issue at hand to lived-in experiences, sometimes her own, at other times, of people she knew and cared about. Mamata, therefore, views domestic violence through the lens of her intense emotions, as a string of terrible tragedies that befell women she had closely worked with and had wanted to protect.

Anguished by the repeated occurrence of violence within the four walls of private and intimate space, Mamata's response, typically, was passionately emotional. 'Despite their zest for life and their energy, Jharna, Anjali and Manju ended their lives under the shadow of their personal tragedies. Several years have gone by since their deaths. But even today their faces are engraved on my heart, their thoughts I carry with me in my innermost recesses. I am pained each time I remember their faces; I do not know when the agony will end. They have ended their physical lives, but will God ever forgive those responsible for their deaths?'[11]

Mamata's negotiation with gender has been mediated by the spirit of welfare and social service. For instance, as a Central minister for women and children, she wanted to improve the condition of sex workers, the 'neglected people' in society. Unlike many feminists, whose analysis of gender-based violence and exploitation is grounded not in victimhood but 'agency', Mamata's approach is traditional, centred on the notion of women as victims. It is interesting to note here that Mamata's perception of herself is as a permanent victim of sorts. Though she has no access to a feminist vocabulary and cannot be ideologically described as one, her emergence as a single-woman leader of lower-middle-class origin fighting with her back to the wall does situate her in a feminist context. Perhaps Mamata's own perception of herself as a woman leader of Opposition in a state known for its political violence, headed by an essentially male establishment, has given her the image of a feminist; though she herself does not perceive herself as one.

A Study in Contrasts

In her own distinctive style, Mamata created a political niche that belonged solely to her, a space she could privilege as her own. As she stepped up protests, controversy trailed her every step of the way. Her combative, in-your-face persona, belligerent style, emotional outpourings, histrionic acts and, last but not the least, her plebeian, unrefined language, all combined to form the 'entity' called Mamata Banerjee. She was almost an affront to West Bengal's bhadralok culture. The middle class looked down their noses at her rustic lack of familiarity with English, her dearth of 'style'. Here was a firebrand MP who challenged the bhadralok's sensibilities of class, language and culture with her otherness. It is odd, of course, that a lower-middle-class, unrefined, non-bourgeois woman symbolized the 'other' in a state ruled by communists.

Plenty of stories about Mamata's flamboyant, melodramatic modus operandi did the rounds: for instance, the time she walked into the Behala police station and sat on the chair of the officer-in-charge; or when unconfirmed reports circulated of her slapping a policeman found guilty of dereliction of duty. On the one hand, Mamata's militancy, a direct counterpoint to the conventional practice of politics, hurt the middle classes' idealized imagination of politicians. She drew contemptuous flak from all quarters. On the other hand, however, Mamata's acts of transgression and her daring evoked admiration among the less sophisticated and underprivileged classes. She had begun to attract a fan following of her own, but she had a long wait of more than a decade before getting wider acceptance as a credible leader of the Opposition and then chief minister.

If we analyse Mamata through the lens of her electoral performance, the impression may tend to be different. Large sections of anti-Left middle classes used to vote for her if only because she was the one consistent force doggedly taking on the ruling CPI-M. Their support for Mamata stemmed more from their aversion to the Left rather than their decisive endorsement of her. To this extent, it may be a mistake to regard electoral results as an indicator of her social and political acceptance in bhadralok society.

'It is now more than eleven years since the Trinamool Congress was formed. The Bengali middle classes for a long time did not accept Mamata Banerjee as an Opposition leader,' Arpita Ghosh said. 'One main reason was her popular, imaginative style of communication, her lack of restraint. Restraint is something the Left and the middle class like. In that sense, Mamata Banerjee is a contrarian politician who articulated her politics differently, who took to the streets, fought, got beaten.' Explaining why, for a long time, the middle class found Mamata cringeworthy, Ghosh said, 'The Left parties have given us our definition of bhadralok—how they should or should not behave, the ideal way to practise politics. CPM and Co. were confident that their definition will hold for ever, preventing Mamata Banerjee's acceptance as a legitimate leader. And they did succeed for a long time. Despite consistently fighting the regime, Mamata Banerjee could not find acceptance till the Singur agitation exploded in the face of the CPI-M in 2006.'

So what larger trend, political and social, did Mamata represent? Or did she scrupulously stick only to her core agenda—her political mission of removing the CPI-M-led regime from power?

A parallel—though admittedly limited—can be drawn between Mamata's ascendancy in West Bengal politics and the emergence of non-gentrified politicians in the Hindi heartland in the post-Mandal era. The implementation of the Mandal Commission report in the early 1990s, for the first time since independence, forced open the gates of Parliament—and public spaces and institutions—to non-elite, non-affluent representatives from the Other Backward Classes. The political and electoral assertion of the Bahujan Samaj Party (BSP) saw more and more Dalit MPs enter Parliament. The character of the Indian Parliament was drastically altered. It may be argued that Mamata represented a popular political consciousness somewhat like the awakening of the underprivileged, which had gone into the making of leaders like Lalu Prasad Yadav, Mulayam Singh Yadav, Kanshi Ram and Mayawati. Like them, Mamata functioned with an entirely different political and social imagination.

The leaders of the backward classes and the Dalits spoke the language of—if not always about the concerns of—the underclass sans conventional frills and niceties. They could strike a rapport and make a connection with ordinary people. Their rhetoric with its mix of crude allegories and homespun fables undoubtedly tapped into the imagination of a large number of people. Despite the common thread of popular consciousness that may bind Mamata with these leaders of social assertion, she is fundamentally different from them. Momentous events like the Mandal Commission Report or even an earlier agitation led by Jayaprakash Narayan had radically impacted the course of Indian politics, not just electorally, but also at a deeper level of social transformation, jolting age-old prejudices of caste.

Mamata's politics was not born of such churnings predicated on a philosophy of social and political change. Her agenda of political transformation was narrow, confined to a transfer of State power and the dislodging of the Left government in West Bengal. If anything, Mamata stood against the grain of the upsurges that had jolted the political establishment at the Centre in the 1970s. An activist of the Congress at the time, Mamata had passionately backed Indira Gandhi and the Emergency. She had militantly opposed Jayaprakash Narayan and the Mandal Commission Report. Unlike Lalu Prasad, Mulayam or Mayawati, before the Singur–Nandigram movements, Mamata had no solid social base of cohesive support, no radicalized constituency of her own.

These differences notwithstanding, it is important to try and locate Mamata within the larger matrix of changes in popular politics that happened in the 1990s. A comparative look at Mamata and Mayawati throws up some interesting insights into the kind of popular politics I am trying to articulate.

India's two prominent women leaders have in common a lack of social and cultural elitism, their eloquence in vernacular languages and their unease with English. And, crucially, their status as single women. Controversies follow them like their own shadows, though for different reasons. Interestingly, these two politicians also stand apart in their striking dissimilarities. On the hierarchy of caste, a potent instrument of discrimination and exploitation, Mamata (a Brahmin) occupies the highest rung, while Mayawati (a Dalit) the lowest. Both were raised in humble surroundings by families that struggled to make ends meet, and both experienced the sting of harsh poverty. Additionally, Mayawati had to contend with an even more formidable hardship—the prejudice of untouchability, the layers of discrimination that ostracize Dalits in every sphere. Both women are well educated and have acquired multiple educational certificates; both have degrees in education and law. Mayawati used to teach in a government school before her mentor Kanshi Ram drew her into full-time politics; Mamata became a full-fledged student activist while she was doing her graduation.

The contrariety between the two leaders is starkest in the way they negotiate their gender identities and assert political and social power. Like Mamata, Mayawati was raised in a large family of six brothers and two sisters, but unlike her, Mayawati faced discrimination as a girl child, early in her life. Perhaps the ill treatment bred defiance in the Dalit leader, leading her to transgress Brahmanical and patriarchal norms. Her relationship with mentor Kanshi Ram illustrated her casual disdain for societal prejudices. Mayawati did not seem to care how the world interpreted her personal relationship. Mamata, on the other hand, has diligently avoided an intimate friendship or relationship with any man. There's an almost puritanical aura about her persona. Clearly, the two women deal with the status of being single very differently.

The list of divergences lengthens further. The BSP leader owed her political roots and her emergence in politics to her tutor and friend Kanshi Ram. Mamata, on the contrary, is entirely self-made, without the hovering presence of a male benefactor in the background. Though single, the personal lives of both women have followed different trajectories. Mayawati continued to live with Kanshi Ram, despite her relationship being a butt of salacious gossip and avid speculation. Mamata, on the other hand, scrupulously maintains her austere image, as if the slightest whiff of romance or even the faintest suggestion of her interest in that area could blight her political image or be construed as straying from the stereotypical 'ideal' notion of a woman.

More intriguing still are the techniques adopted by these two powerful leaders to assert their political and social supremacy. Frugality is the essence of Mamata's lifestyle. She maintains a calibrated Spartan personal appearance, doubtless in large part as a method of combating the communists who are known for their austerity. Her look is simple: plain cotton saris and an overall grounded, earthy feel. Her only pieces of jewellery are a thin chain around her neck and inconspicuous ear studs. In contrast we have Mayawati, bedecked in diamonds, an image of ostentation. If austerity is a dominant marker of Mamata's personality, a blatant display of wealth is Mayawati's hallmark. In matters of financial honesty, the Trinamool Congress chief is believed to be above reproach; she is even known to pay for her tea in the railway ministry. The chief minister of Uttar Pradesh is facing multiple charges and allegations of corruption. Last year, the railway minister's assets approximated ₹6.7 lakh,[12] while Mayawati's, as she declared them at the time of filing her nomination for the upper house of the Uttar Pradesh assembly the same year, were to the tune of ₹87.2 crore.[13]

But these defining characteristics of the two women—frugality and ostentation—needs to be understood within their own specific cultural, social and political contexts. The Trinamool chief's political lineage is tied to the Congress. While most of the party's leaders can hardly profess to be Gandhian in their politics or their lifestyles, the party does claim Mahatma Gandhi as part of its lineage. This 'Gandhian' space—I use the term in a limited sense—seems to have been occupied by Mamata. Her austerity is an important aspect of her 'Gandhian' way of living—as is her dress code. Political theorist Aditya Nigam contrasts Mayawati's ostentatious style with Gandhi's subdued, understated one—encapsulated in khadi, a coarse homespun cloth, usually white. Nigam points out that Gandhi's discarding of Western clothes on his return from South Africa and his taking to wearing the loincloth was 'an act of affiliation with the large and poverty-stricken masses of Indians'.[14]

White is regarded as the colour of sacrifice, honesty and purity in the Hindu religion: the colour Mamata has chosen to identify with. Her saris are always unfailingly white with a thin coloured border. Through her Gandhian attire, sparse lifestyle, a deliberate shunning of accessories denoting rank and status, Mamata seems to convey her identification with the poor and her refusal to embrace a standard of living that would widen the chasm between her and the ordinary people whom she wants to represent. Asked by a reporter why she always wore rubber slippers, Mamata replied that she simply liked wearing them. Of course, there is the argument that her sartorial choices and her way of living are little more than an exercise to craft an image.

Mayawati, on the other hand, represents a distinctly 'anti-Gandhian' stream of political consciousness shaped by Dalit icon B.R. Ambedkar. Unlike Gandhi, Ambedkar was always in a Western suit, his attire a manifestation of his deeper philosophy. Mayawati's style—loud, ostentatious and in-your-face—may be interpreted as her and her community's way of asserting power, of defying spatial, cultural and political segregation. According to Nigam, 'Mayawati's "ostentatiousness" and her sartorial preferences can be read as her symbolic countermove that mocks Gandhi's attempts at representing poverty and mourning through the semiotic transformation of his body. If Gandhi, the baniya, had to display the poverty and suffering he never actually experienced, here was Mayawati, a representative of the really poor and oppressed, by her very appearance ridiculing that attempt, much like Ambedkar's Western suit did.'[15] With her short hair, flashy clothes and jewellery, Mayawati could hardly have been more strikingly different from Mamata in her white sari, her long hair pulled back into a traditional bun and her trademark rubber chappals.

Their personal styles, so remarkably distinct from each other, seem to articulate two different languages of politics for reclaiming spaces. Through her politics of Dalit empowerment, Mayawati symbolizes the aspirations of many in her community. By contrast, Mamata's image is not rooted in a community in this sense, but in her everlasting desire to find a language of politics adequate for defeating the CPI-M.

At the same time, Mamata has seen up close the prejudices driven by a deep-rooted class bias. She felt its cut more deeply on entering the Lok Sabha, after joining the ranks of the privileged. 'There are some members whose appearance may lack smartness, who do not speak English with the anglicized accent, but these members are very active and make honest attempts to speak for the welfare of the people. However, these members rarely get the opportunity,' she writes, going on to say that: 'It occurs to me repeatedly that members are divided into two distinct classes. There is a special group of members who, while addressing the Chair, keep their main focus on the Press Gallery, for the sake of publicity. The other "ordinary" class lacks "glamour", hence they are less important. It seems that they are there to mark their presence only. This makes me feel very sad and reminds me of the concept of "first class citizen" and "second class citizen".'[16]

The Personal is Political

It is by now axiomatic that, for Mamata, the personal is the political—in fact, the 'personal' has often threatened to swamp and destabilize the 'political'. It is impossible to situate Mamata within the contemporary political grid without citing a few of the many unusual ways she chose to express her emotions—angst, anger, irritation. Even today, she bears the cross of having allowed her emotions to control her political language and means of protest. Still, there is a touch of perverse humour to these incidents.

Krishna Bose remembers the day when Mamata, in a fit of roiling anger, caught hold of Samajwadi Party MP Daroga Prasad Saroj by the scruff of his collar and virtually dragged him out of the well of the Lok Sabha. Saroj was trying to wrestle the Women's Reservation Bill down, ready to physically attack its supporters. Saroj and the others who opposed the bill were every bit as wild as Mamata in their methods of protest. We aren't likely to forget those visuals in a hurry: irate members, prodded by their seniors in the Rashtriya Janata Dal and Samajwadi Party, tearing the bill to shreds, stomping around the well of the House.

Krishna Bose also recalls that the incident was stamped with a Mamata-brand of hilarity: 'I was a well-behaved MP, never in favour of rushing to the well of the House. The contentious Women's Reservation Bill was going to be placed in the Lok Sabha that day. Mamata was then president of the Trinamool Congress. As usual, the bill sparked a commotion. Mamata had told me we should go to the front. Since I do not believe in agitating in the well of the House, I stood near my seat. Suddenly, I noticed Mamata's shawl was missing. A scuffle was going on inside the well of the House. I asked Akbar Khondakar to go and see what was happening. By then Mamata already had the Samajwadi Party MP by his collar!' On her way back from Parliament that evening, Krishna Bose told Mamata that, as president of a political party, she should show restraint even when the provocation was grave. 'We know how childlike Mamata can be. She told me, "But Krishna-di, the MP tripped me and I fell. I thought I would get a grip on his hair and get up. But on reaching out for his head I discovered he was bald! It was only then that I caught him by his collar."' Her trademark mischievousness was clearly still intact.

On another occasion, Krishna Bose remembers Mamata flinging her shawl at then railway minister Ram Vilas Paswan, angry with what she perceived as discrimination against West Bengal in Paswan's railway budget. 'The shawl missed Paswan, fell on Mulayam Singh Yadav, who then placed it in front of Santosh Mohan Dev. He in turn came and gave it to me. I folded it neatly and kept it on my desk.' Mamata was by then sitting in a dharna.

The famous 'black shawl', flung so often with disdain, had transcended into a metaphor for a reprimanding staff. Mamata leveraged her shawl as a potent instrument to cow down her adversaries. Nagged by the anxiety of an unholy camaraderie brewing between the party she belonged to and the party she had vowed to unseat, Mamata in 1996 chose a rally to stage one of her thespian moments. At a public gathering in Kolkata's Alipore, she wrapped her black shawl, by now undisputedly an intimidating piece of clothing, around her neck. Protesting the Congress's 'underhand dealings' with the CPI-M, she threatened to tie her shawl into a suicidal noose. Predictably she had her moment in the media, and the incident was lodged in the collective memory as yet another of Mamata's histrionic attempts at grabbing attention—one more testimony to Mamata's seemingly unstable, deeply conflicted personality, always riding high on emotions.

The other accessory that gave serious competition to the black shawl was Mamata's jhola, a cotton bag she always carried. 'The shoulder bag was like my own family. I could stuff it with every possible item of use. It was really functional,' she writes.[17] The most useful item in the jhola was a first aid kit. Like Mayawati's handbag, displayed prominently on her statues and perceived to be a symbol of her power and Dalit assertion, Mamata's jhola, synonymous with West Bengal's radical political, intellectual culture, seemed to signify her bonding with the state and its people.

Before ending this chapter, it is perhaps worth mentioning the fact that Mayawati and Mamata—both theatrical and spectacular in their own ways—have also often been accused of 'opportunism' in their politics. Opponents have pointed to the alliance that both women and their parties have had with the BJP, thus supposedly undermining their credentials as progressive political leaders. But, interestingly, neither Mayawati nor Mamata really 'lost out' politically because of these alliances, successfully distancing themselves from the 'Hindutva' tag in popular imagination.

It may be useful at this juncture to examine the extent to which allegations of this sort miss the complicated politics that Mayawati and Mamata inhabit. Both have clear political 'goals'.

For Mayawati, this is connected intrinsically to Dalit politics; while, for Mamata, dislodging the CPI-M is the only political aim of any worth. Of course, dislodging the CPI-M means much more than simple political change: it is also an overhauling of the whole set of cultural, political and social values that are ingrained in the decaying bhadralok culture of contemporary West Bengal.

4

The Singur–Nandigram–Lalgarh Journey

At 7.30 a.m. on 18 December 2006, Mamata Banerjee heard of the murder of sixteen-year-old Tapasi Malik, an activist in the Singur agitation. At that time, the Trinamool leader was on an indefinite fast protesting coercive land acquisition in Singur. The agitation against handing over 1,000 acres of fertile multi-crop land to the Tatas for their Nano factory, where they would build the cheapest car in India, was spreading like wildfire.

'I am writing this from the podium where I have been on fast. Here I learnt at 7.30 on the morning of the 18th that Tapasi Malik, who till yesterday was on fast with the rest of the protestors in Singur, has been raped and murdered earlier this morning at five. [...] I spoke to Tapasi's brother from the podium. I was told that despite the presence of the family, the police had rushed the body to hospital. Immediately, I urged Trinamool MP Mukul Roy, leader of the Opposition Partha Chatterjee, and Amitabha Bhattacharya to leave for the spot so that the police and CPI-M cannot brush the incident under the carpet,' Mamata wrote.[1]

Terror was stalking Singur. Activists were being intimidated and thrashed; some, like Rajkumar Bhulu and Tapasi Malik, were killed. Tapasi's murder stunned the people of West Bengal, giving the Singur agitation a razor-sharp edge. Civil society members, intellectuals, artistes, political activists of all stripes and NGO activists all joined in.

Mamata demanded a CBI inquiry into the murder. She finally had her way, but not before the CPI-M had launched a smear campaign, accusing Tapasi's father of raping her. A look at the CPI-M's rhetoric during this period may help us understand the dynamics of the Singur upsurge—a phenomenon that marked the beginning of Mamata's ascendance in West Bengal politics.

Within three years of her Singur struggle, Mamata found an acceptance among all sections and classes of people that far exceeded her own expectation. She was finally the 'real' face of a political alternative. The more the CPI-M railed against the Trinamool Congress, the more people perceived Mamata as their deliverer from an arrogant ruling coalition. To understand her swift and dramatic transition from an erratic leader to a people's person who could transcend barriers of class, culture and politics, we must revisit those three crucial years, 2006 to 2009.

By then, their backs to the wall on the Singur issue, the communists were lashing out. Much of the rhetoric—its lack of gender sensitivity for instance—would have been only too familiar to Mamata. Here is an example of the party's vocabulary following Tapasi's murder, from an article in the CPI-M mouthpiece *People's Democracy*:

> The Central Bureau of Investigation (CBI) probing the case now believes that the young woman's father and brother might have had something to do with her murder.
>
> Tapasi's death had been utilized shamelessly and to the hilt by the Naxalites, the SUCI initially, then followed up by

the Trinamul Congress, the Pradesh Congress, and the BJP, to try to embarrass the CPI(M) and the Bengal Left Front government.[2]

B. Prasant, author of the article, went on to say: 'In all probability, the duo [Tapasi's father Monoranjan and brother Surajit] will be subjected to sophisticated probing techniques, such as narco-analysis, brain-mapping and DNA testing. The blood samples taken from the murder site apparently do not match the samples of blood collected from Monoranjan and Surajit. The father-and-son may also be subjected to a "lie-detector" or "polygraph" test. The CBI has no doubt that young Tapasi Malik was killed in planned manner and that the story runs much deeper than what appearances would tell.'

A month later, the CBI arrested Suhrid Datta, secretary of the CPI-M Zonal Committee in Singur, and Debu Malik, a CPI-M supporter, in connection with Tapasi's rape and murder. In 2008, the Chandannagar sub-divisional court sentenced both Suhrid and Debu to life imprisonment. Next year, the Calcutta High Court released Suhrid on bail, and jubilant CPI-M supporters organized a victory rally to celebrate their leader's release.

Mamata's Resurrection

West Bengal entered a new phase of its political history in 2006. The catalysts were Singur, Nandigram and, later, Lalgarh. Mamata stood at the threshold of a momentous phase of politics.

These developments impacted the quality of Mamata's politics, moulding and transforming it. Her political plans had not involved becoming the nerve centre of movements of the calibre of Singur and Nandigram, with such far-reaching political and economic implications. But an unforeseen turn of events led her to this unfamiliar arena of peasants' struggles, a quintessential feature of communist politics, a preserve of the Left. A qualitative shift marked Mamata's transition from a theatrical activist to a figure around whom leaders, intellectuals, activists and artistes rallied. Even the well heeled, so far suspicious of her subaltern and unpolished ways, now began to view her with interest, if not admiration.

The exit of the Tatas from Singur provoked political and economic pundits to pronounce Mamata's doom. They said she'd be perceived as driving industrialization out of a state that was economically stagnant and in desperate need of industries. However, Mamata continued to gain electoral ground. The middle classes, dismayed though they were over the collapse of the Nano project and the exit of the Tatas, voted for the Trinamool Congress in the municipal elections. Even the middle-class Salt Lake area went the Mamata way. Clearly, anger against the Left exceeded innate reservations of class, politics and culture that in the past had weighed Mamata Banerjee down.

Today, most commentators, at least at the national level, believe that the continuum of movements—beginning with Singur, gaining ground at Nandigram, and then flowing into the tribal upsurge at Lalgarh—had their genesis in the Trinamool Congress and Mamata Banerjee. Without a doubt, Mamata—who had been virtually written off until then—was the most effective beneficiary of the movements. The pertinent question though is: did the movements 'make' Mamata Banerjee? Or did she 'make' them?

The CPI-M rhetoric is that these struggles are part of a Trinamool–Maoist conspiracy to derail industrialization and destabilize the progressive, secular, democratic (the Left Front's three pet words) government.

But to return to our examination of the significance of these events in Mamata's political life. There have been many catalytic agents in Mamata's career: 1984, the victory against Somnath Chatterjee; 1990, the Hazra junction attack; 1998, founding the Trinamool; 1999, her appointment as railway minister. Like Singur and Nandigram, each one of these developments had been a marker of radical change in Mamata's career. She defeated the veteran CPI-M MP when she was only twenty-nine years old and in the first lap of her political journey. The attack at Hazra junction on 16 August 1990 stamped her with the image of a bleeding victim, an incredibly brave woman, battling almost single-handedly, even if in vain, the CPI-M's indomitable organization and state machinery. Mamata's appointment as minister of railways marked her presence in West Bengal in a significantly different fashion, not just as the CPI-M's aggressive combatant, but also as West Bengal's 'very own' railway minister.

But the significance of Singur-Nandigram—coming as it did in the wake of the Left Front's stunning electoral victory in 2006 and the Trinamool's utter rout—was of another magnitude altogether. Between 2006 and 2009, the peasant movements changed all that, reinventing the Trinamool Congress, resurrecting and re-energizing its leader. All of a sudden, Mamata, went from being the chastened Opposition leader to becoming the most formidable contestant for power that the Left had ever tackled. Singur-Nandigram recast the image of the Trinamool, lending it the political content it sorely lacked. Crucially, the Trinamool breached the Left's political territory, representing itself as a party of peasants and the underclass. As events unfolded, the party acquired a fundamentally new image, almost as if it had morphed into a new political entity.

In the past, Mamata Banerjee's popularity had stemmed from her aura: her lower-middle-class background, her humble residence in a run-down area of Kolkata and her deliberate shunning of accoutrements of privilege. The Trinamool Congress leader seemed to stand out in her sheer ordinariness. But none of this helped her break through to the Left-leaning bhadralok activists, artistes and intellectuals. Not long ago, comments like 'you do not entrust the maid with the keys to your house' could commonly be heard in Kolkata. The radical, anti-establishment character of the bhadralok has always coexisted with a deep social and political conservatism. So even those sections of the bhadralok that were anti-CPI-M did not automatically accept Mamata.

For all of these reasons, 2006 was a watershed in Mamata Banerjee's political career. Armed with her breakthrough experience of popular political movements, the Trinamool president could now negotiate political business with the CPI-M from a position of strength. She was no longer an inconsequential, muddle-headed adversary.

The change in the political barometer was evident, and Mamata was now pulling off one electoral coup after another. Even her rhetoric was more than just emotional outbursts now. Many argue that, during this period, she acquired the political language and the idiom of the Left. For instance, her slogan 'Maa, Maati, Manush' was essentially born out of the struggles in Singur and Nandigram, each word drawing attention to a different aspect of the emotional-political charge of those movements:

'Maa' synonymous with Bengal, which to Mamata, was always supreme; 'Maati' standing for 'land' not just in an economic sense, but as something people are wedded to, around which their lives revolve; 'Manush' referring to humanity, to humanism, which Mamata believes to be her only political ideology in the face of brutal state repression and killing.

Peasant struggles, Mamata well knew, were what had given Left politics in West Bengal its unique identity. In *Andoloner Katha*, a collection of essays, Mamata seems to have imbibed—if not outright appropriated—the Left's polemics on liberalization and the need for an alternative trajectory of development. She writes: 'In the name of development, unethical and unprincipled professional politicians-turned-businessmen are out to sell the country's education, civilization, culture and economy.'[3] Again: 'Truly, the development of twenty people is today the primary objective of politicians. Why should they think of the concerns of millions of people? They have to think of just those twenty inordinately wealthy people. [...] They call it industrialization, but it is actually a narrative of destruction'[4]

Suddenly, Mamata's party of 'non-intellectuals' started drawing to its fold a large number of Left-wing academics, intellectuals, artistes. A section of the Left-oriented disenchanted voters began to seriously consider the Trinamool Congress as a viable electoral alternative. Many, however, still held out in the early days of turbulence. 'More than Nandigram, Singur made a qualitative difference to the party,' says a senior Trinamool Congress leader, adding: 'It was the first in the series of movements that changed the political landscape.'

But Nandigram and Singur were certainly not the first time that Mamata had led agitations or mobilized huge crowds. If anything, fasts and dharnas were her most tested forms of agitation. For instance, human rights activists speak of her twenty-four-day dharna at Dharamtala against deaths in police custody. So what lent the Singur movement its special quality? In Mamata's words: 'I have agitated in the past; I have seen huge gatherings on the Brigade Parade Ground on 21 July as well as on other occasions. There would be a sea of people, but just on that one day. But never before have I seen a constant stream of people for so many days. Do remember, this place is really far and not easily accessible. It is difficult to reach the spot and stay here.'[5]

It's true that Mamata gained immeasurably from these agitations then. But she did not 'make' them. Though Singur and Nandigram—even Lalgarh—are often tied to the Trinamool Congress, the reality is somewhat different. The roots of these resistances were scattered, not concentrated in one single individual or party. To the CPI-M, the diverse people in the movements were simply 'outsiders' (interestingly a term which was also used recently by Libyan President Col. Gaddafi against protesters demanding liberty in Libya). The CPI-M either failed to or refused to recognize the unusual character of these movements. Before we go on, it is important to outline the broad contours of the Singur-Nandigram movements to understand the context for the re-emergence of Mamata.

STORMING THE COMMUNIST BASTION

In the initial stages of the Singur movement, the Trinamool Congress's contribution was confined to the active role played by Rabindranath Bhattacharya, the party's local MLA. 'It was everybody's movement. The Singur Krishi Jami Raksha

Committee [SKJRC] was heading the agitation, which included the SUCI and various factions of Marxist-Leninist parties,' Pradip Banerjee, who headed the SKJRC for a while, told me.

In the words of singer-songwriter Kabir Suman, who was elected to Parliament on a Trinamool ticket in the 2009 general elections, 'The huge setback the Left suffered since 2006 was not due to any particular political party or leadership. The credit goes to the people of Bengal and the role of grambanglar jhanta (the broomstick of rural Bengal).'[6]

Leaders of political parties as well as members of non-political organizations started arriving at Singur following a gherao of the district magistrate and the block division officer on 25 September 2006. The protesters wanted to prevent 'fake' claimants from picking up the compensation cheques for the land acquired in the area. 'Leaders and individuals—Mamata Banerjee, Saugata Roy, Asim Chatterjee, Barnali Mukherjee, Naba Datta—started arriving at the site of the dharna,' Pradip Banerjee recounts. The police mounted a brutal attack, arresting over seventy women, including a two-and-a-half-year-old girl. Historian Kunal Chattopadhyay wrote: 'A little after midnight, a blackout was created, and under the cover of darkness, a huge police force, according to the victims well lubricated with alcohol, attacked and brutally beat up the protestors, men, women and children. Ms Banerjee was also manhandled, and her sari torn. She was then bundled off to Kolkata by force, and had to be admitted to a hospital.'[7] This attack escalated the tempo of the agitation. Mamata was emerging as the political and electoral symbol of the agitation. But even then, the SKJRC, the nerve centre of the movement and a platform of diverse non-partisan groups and individuals, enjoyed a great deal of autonomy in decision making.

'All parties were invited—Subrata Mukherjee, then a Congress leader, Anuradha Talwar and Swapan Ganguly of the Paschim Banga Khet Mazdoor Samiti, Saifuddin Chowdhury and Samir Putatunda of the Party for Democratic Socialism,' says Pradip Banerjee. After police attacked and arrested delegates on their way to Singur to attend an open convention, the range of participants widened. 'We then approached the Congress, the breakaway Forward Bloc, Janata Dal (Secular), and Samajwadi Party to join the movement,' adds Banerjee. Mamata began her fast on 4 December 2006, on a podium near Kolkata's Metro Channel, in protest against the police action.

In *Nishaaner Naam Tapasi Malik*, his recently published best-selling book, Kabir Suman traces the beginning of his journey with Mamata as a participant in the Singur movement: 'Mamata Banerjee had begun her fast. Abhash Munshi from the Mazdoor Kranti Parishad, Bijoy Upadhyay, president of the Samajwadi Party's West Bengal unit, and radical activist Barnali Upadhyay had also joined her.' Suman was then working with the current affairs programme at Tara News channel. 'On the TV monitor, I saw CPI-M leaders addressing the media. A CPI-M leader cracked a joke about Mamata Banerjee getting hurt in the police attack at Singur. In full camera glare he said, "Why does she get hurt on her chest so much?" He kept repeating the ugly comment. I made up my mind, deciding to go to the spot where Mamata was fasting, to show my solidarity with her.'[8]

Suman describes his first face-to-face encounter with Mamata thus: 'This was the first time I saw Mamata from close quarters and spoke with her. Exhausted from fasting, she was lying down, wrapped in a blanket. She tried to get up on seeing me and would not heed my protests. We had a brief conversation. She spoke in a low but spirited tone. I told her, "I have come here in solidarity. I am concerned about your health." Folding her hands in gratitude, she said, "Please do not worry. I will continue my fast."[9]

But Bengal's intellectuals and artistes were still hesitant about sharing a podium with Mamata. 'How many artistes and intellectuals had gone to the fasting site?' asks Suman. Mahasweta Devi was one of the first ones to visit her and express solidarity. 'For a long time, I have noticed the "keep-away-from Mamata" attitude. I really cannot claim that I myself was totally free from it. Truthfully, I did not like her alliance with the BJP; I could not accept its continuation even after the massacre of Muslims in Gujarat by Hindu fascists,' is Suman's candid confession.[10] Rather than shun the sceptics, Mamata waited her turn, which arrived at the end of the Singur–Nandigram–Lalgarh journey. Finally, she seemed to have whittled down the reservations of the large group of intellectuals and artistes. They were now firmly by her side.

The initial activity around land acquisition in Singur didn't breach the barrier totally. In fact, after a point, the noise died down. Then in 2007, Nandigram erupted when police opened fire on protestors there. The long saga of the pitched battle in Nandigram seemed to re-infuse energy across the rest of the state. By 2008, Singur was on the boil again, and in the long run it would be Singur that would tip the scales politically in the state. In August 2008, dramatic scenes unfolded along the Durgapur Expressway. Different political parties and organizations set up twenty-one camps on the side of the road. Earlier, in 2006, Mamata had gone on a twenty-six-day hunger strike, demanding that the state government return 400 acres of land to the peasants of Singur. The finale to the tussle over the Nano project in Singur had begun.

'Leaders, workers and, above all, people are staying here through day and night. [...] People are bringing a handful of rice and dal for all the satyagrahis. MLA Rabinbabu is supervising the cooking of khichri. As soon as dawn breaks, the volunteers get down to work, cleaning the area. A total of twenty-one camps: the first one supervised by Mukul [Mukul Roy] and the twenty-first by Bani Sinha Roy.' This was Mamata's description of those days.[11]

The movement had its own brand of 'Mamata aesthetics' as she sat with an easel on the podium and applied her paintbrushes to canvas. Some people sang Rabindrasangeet and others sang songs of the revolutionary IPTA composer Salil Chowdhury. Meanwhile, hectic negotiations were under way inside Raj Bhavan. Upon Mamata's request, Governor Gopalkrishna Gandhi, the mediator, was trying to find a face-saver for the Left Front government; a last-minute unravelling of the hopelessly tangled plot of Singur. But the intractable deadlock remained in place as firmly. Finally, the Tatas packed up and left. The Nano, supposed to have been a feather in the CPI-M government's worn-out crown, lay in tatters.

'The CPI-M transferred the entire blame for the situation to the Opposition. According to them, Mamata Banerjee had prevented West Bengal's industrialization. To me, that explanation is not acceptable,' says Abhirup Sarkar, an economist at Kolkata's Indian Statistical Institute. Sarkar is close to Mamata and was at one point rumoured to be in the running for the post of finance minister in the Trinamool government. Though Sarkar did not accept her offer to contest the polls, he continues to be an advisor to Mamata. He points to data from the manufacturing sector to shore up his arguments: 'West Bengal's industrial decline had started from the 1980s. In this period, the state's contribution to the all-India manufacturing sector was a little less than 13 per cent. In 2009, that figure stood at a little above 2 per cent. In the 1980s, only four states—Maharashtra and Gujarat (the industrially advanced), and Punjab and Haryana (the agriculturally prosperous)—were ahead of us. Now the entire south and Himachal Pradesh have overtaken us; soon Rajasthan will too. Industrial decline was an ongoing process. It did not suddenly dip because the Singur project could not take off.'

So does he give no credence to the argument that Mamata forcefully stalled the Nano project? 'When Mamata Banerjee began her opposition she had no political support. In 2006, she could not have stopped the Singur project forcefully, simply because she hardly had any political power then. In fact, things worked the other way: the Singur movement made Mamata Banerjee powerful,' Sarkar suggests. Many have argued that the West Bengal government could have neutralized the resistance had it drawn up a better compensation deal. Perhaps—but even that would not have worked if the government had gone ahead and terrorized people, hoping to bully them into submission. Sarkar draws an interesting parallel between the experiences of peasants in Singur and Mexico City.

In 2002, a proposal was mooted to build a second airport outside Mexico City. Land belonging to peasants had to be acquired. There was resistance to the project. The compensation that was initially offered fell far below expectations, and to add salt to injury, the police beat up and arrested resistance leaders. Eventually, popular discontent forced the government to offer a huge compensation amount. But the peasants refused. 'The lesson from here and Singur is that we are dealing with human beings, not robots,' Sarkar says. He argues that the resistance in Singur met with a similar aggressive, violent response from the government. 'At first they beat up people, raped women and then they offered more money. Why should [the people] take it?'

He describes the experience of working on a project in Singur as being straight out of a film. 'I went to Singur with a couple of economists doing a project in the area. During our work—just like in Bengali films—two men came on a motorbike, followed by three chamchas and started heckling us.' The men, from the CPI-M cadre, were suspicious of 'outsiders' and obstructed their work. This intimidation of perceived outsiders is characteristic of the CPI-M's politics, its constant distrust of those who are not its own. Sarkar's comparison to scenes like this in popular Bengali cinema is quite apt. In many a popular film, the damsel in distress or the hero is attacked by hooligans who work for the villain—often a rich landowner or member of the bourgeoisie, and sometimes of an unnamed 'party'!

The Singur saga played out over two years—from 2006 (when a confident Left Front government acquired the land) to 2008 (when the Tatas finally left). And when the Singur crisis seemed to have reached a point of stasis, Nandigram exploded, an explosion that revitalized the final stages of the Singur movement as well.

In 2006, Chief Minister Buddhadeb Bhattacharjee handed over 14,000 acres of land in Nandigram to Indonesia's Salim Group of industries to set up a chemical hub. Like in Singur, the CPI-M looked the other way while resentment simmered and a Bhumi Uchchhed Pratirodh Committee (Committee against Eviction from Land) was set up. For almost a year, people were left to speculate in the dark, uncertain and apprehensive about the ramifications of the decision. The government operated with a total lack of transparency and made no attempt to initiate a democratic dialogue on the process of acquisition. Despite arm-twisting by Lakshman Seth, CPI-M's powerful MP in the area, the peasants threw their weight behind the forces of resistance. They drove CPI-M workers out of Nandigram, until then a party stronghold. The violence that CPI-M workers unleashed against the protesters is by now well known. The best known of these incidents occurred on 14 March 2007, when the police—among them a section of CPI-M workers masquerading as policemen—brutally attacked peasants, unintentionally 'creating' a mass movement.

Singur and Nandigram shared many similarities, among them the diversity of the participants in these struggles. Mamata did not personally intervene in the initial stages of the agitations. Trinamool Congress MLA Shubhendhu Adhikari was at the forefront of the Nandigram movement alongside activists from many other organizations and parties. The presence of activists from various factions of Marxist-Leninist parties gave the CPI-M fodder for its 'Mamata–Maoist nexus' campaign, which reached its height in the wake of the Lalgarh crisis.

Nandigram fortified Mamata Banerjee's image. Her colleagues and fellow activists from those days recall 14 March 2007 with special clarity. At Mamata's Kalighat residence, everybody was on their mobile phone. News of a savage attack by CPI-M cadres and policemen in Nandigram had thrown them into a tizzy. Mamata was talking to journalists. She had decided to go to Nandigram. On her way, she spoke to leaders of the Congress and the BJP, including L.K. Advani. But nobody seemed to have a clue about how to rein the CPI-M in. Kabir Suman, who was travelling in a car with Mamata then, writes:

I notice the Congress is not paying that much heed. Where is the prime minister? He must know what is happening here. Why can he not call up Buddhadeb Bhattacharjee and ask him to stop the rape and murder? Then, does everyone want such chaos to continue in West Bengal?

At Mecheda, the CPI-M stopped our convoy. Mamata's car was right in front. Sitting right behind her, I could see what kind of lewd gestures the party cadres were making at Mamata… In that crowd there were boys, men—both young and old—and women too. I cannot believe that such terrible, ugly comments can be made targeting a woman. Mamata sat furious. After continuing like this for a long time, the cadres moved away.[12]

In the evening, Mamata reached Tamluk hospital, where the wounded had been brought. Some grievously injured, some dying. Mamata was by the side of a woman with a bullet in her lower stomach. As cameras zeroed in on the scene, Mamata pulled up the media. Subrata Mukherjee arrived at the hospital fighting attacks on his car by CPI-M workers. Mamata, despite repeated warnings of danger, was determined to go to Nandigram that very night. She was stalled finally by a barricade set up by a massive CPI-M contingent. It took a great deal of persuasion to get Mamata to turn back. The one quality that impressed and widened Mamata's circle of friends, supporters and colleagues was her courage and fearlessness. Some of them say that her years of life-threatening combat with the CPI-M had left her virtually without fear of death. For Abhirup Sarkar, Mamata's persona is a combination of three 'sha-s'. 'I would describe Mamata Banerjee's personality as a sum total of Bengali shahas (courage), shatata (honesty) and sharalya (simplicity),' he says.

The Singur and Nandigram movements worked at many

levels. Primarily, they sparked an 'audacity of hope', says Sujato Bhadra, playing on Barack Obama's famous phrase. 'Mamata Banerjee has become a symbol of change,' he told me. 'Paribartan', a word that had fallen out of Bengal's political dictionary, was now on everybody's lips. Amid the churnings, Mamata gained some unexpected allies, many of them from the Leftist political stream. Sections of the Marxist-Leninist factions in the state were one such group. Their intrinsic suspicion of Mamata broke down when they saw her grit and involvement in Singur, Nandigram and, later, Lalgarh. Mamata's association with Marxist-Leninist parties, inconceivable even a few years ago, firmed up during 2006–09. Some, like Purnendu Bose and Dola Sen, who formally joined the Trinamool Congress, are now among her closest political aides. Others, like Pradip Banerjee, did not join Mamata's party, but did actively campaign for her in the assembly elections. But the political Left wasn't the only force that took a sudden interest in Mamata, as we shall see in the next chapter.

Mamata and the Maoists

Following the epic confrontations in Singur and Nandigram, a third rebellion gathered force in the tribal districts of rural Bengal, for long repressed by an uncaring establishment and an indifferent state.

In Lalgarh, in the West Medinipur district of West Bengal, the tribal people began agitating in the winter of 2008. It was an exemplary struggle—democratic and diverse—till the Maoists wrested control of the movement and the joint Central and state forces occupied the region known as Jangalmahal. In the initial stages, like in Singur and Nandigram, many different organizations and political parties gathered and functioned democratically under the Pulishi Santrash Birodhi Janasadharaner Committee (People's Committee against Police Atrocities). Later, the Maoists hijacked the movement, stifling it before the resisting tribals could achieve some of their basic demands.

The genesis of the Lalgarh resistance was a bomb blast on 2 November 2008, targeting a high-profile Central and state delegation, including Chief Minister Buddhadeb Bhattacharjee. They narrowly escaped with their lives from the blast set up by Maoists in Shalboni. In spite of extensive reconnaissance before the delegation's arrival, the police had failed to detect the long wire that set off the ambush. To make up for this major lapse, the police began a massive hunt for the culprits, with savage reprisals on the tribals. But inhabitants of this region had long been familiar with police brutality. And from about 2000, the Maoists too were gaining influence in the poverty-ridden areas of Jangalmahal, including the three most backward districts, Purulia, Medinipur and Bankura.

The success of the peasant movements in Singur and Nandigram inspired the restless tribals of Lalgarh to teach the uncaring government a lesson. Mamata Banerjee became part of the upsurge much later. In fact, she was allowed to join a rally of the People's Committee against Police Atrocities (PCPA) on condition that she would not carry a Trinamool Congress banner.

In *Andoloner Katha*, Mamata recounts her memory of Lalgarh as she had seen it in 1992 when she was criss-crossing West Bengal, trying to revive the Congress through her interactions with people. She began her month-long journey from Belpahari in West Medinipur on 12 January, coinciding with Vivekananda's birthday. 'I got news of the desperate plight of the adivasis—nine out of twelve months a year, they cannot get rice. I decided to visit an adivasi village. Without informing anyone, I hitched a ride with a local boy on his scooter and reached Jeb, an adivasi village. With us, some friends in the media also reached the spot,' she writes.[13]

In the village she met women who, she claims, cooked a broth of red ants with roots of trees for food. 'I not only raised the plight of the adivasis at public meetings, but also brought it to the notice of the government so that justice could be done. Sections of the media also put out the news. But the suffering of the adivasis still continues,' Mamata says in the book.[14] Mahasweta Devi remembers Mamata as a co-fighter in her battle against the Left Front government on behalf of the de-notified tribes. 'She helped me when I filed a case against the state government,' the author-activist told me.

Mamata's association with the Lalgarh movement sharpened the Left's accusation that the Trinamool was colluding with the Maoists, an allegation that went back to the days of the Nandigram agitation. While in Lalgarh, the Maoists did have a dominant presence even before they took over the movement lock, stock and barrel, in Nandigram the Trinamool–Maoist nexus might have been just a flight of CPI-M fancy. Without going into the intricacies of a movement as complex and diverse as Lalgarh—at least when it first started—various sections branded the PCPA as a Maoist front and its leader Chhatradhar Mahato as a Maoist agent. Mamata's meeting with Mahato was touted as incontrovertible proof of a Trinamool–Maoist nexus, as was Mahato's membership of the Trinamool in his younger days. By the same logic, film actors, authors, poets and artistes who had gone to Lalgarh and spoken to Mahato were said to be helping the Maoist cause.

In all that noise, no one bothered to question the clear disconnect between the politics of the Maoists and the Trinamool Congress. The media too seemed content to club *all* anti-Left agitators as Maoists of one sort or another. It is important here to make a distinction between the democratic politics of the various Marxist-Leninist parties, which played a crucial role in the Singur and Nandigram agitations, and the project of violent overthrow of the Indian state as espoused by the Maoists. Some people from the Marxist-Leninist parties who had worked closely with Mamata in Singur and Nandigram even switched loyalties to align firmly with the Trinamool.

'One afternoon Mamata telephoned me. She seemed agitated. She told me, "I don't know, Kabir-da, in this situation created by the CPI-M, how long we can practise democracy in this state. I will take one more chance, then I will take up arms,"' Kabir Suman says in his book, adding: 'Considering the situation from all aspects, my mental state was also similar. How can I take up arms at my age? Yet I felt, to hell with everything. What is the point of living like this?'[15]

The CPI-M pounced on this section of Suman's book, splashing it across its party organ, *Ganashakti*, and pointing to it as a confirmation of their theory of Trinamool–Maoist nexus. If you care to read till the end of the page, however, you find this: 'I concede that, given the state of my mind, Mamata's suggestion of taking up arms touched a chord in me. At that point, I did believe Mamata was my comrade, one of us. [...] I do agree there was certain romanticism in that thought. But can you fight a battle without any romanticism?'[16]

Battling the establishment, particularly through armed insurrection, has always carried with it a certain aura of romance, the dangerous bravura of staring death in the face. Che Guevara, now heavily marketed the world over by multinational companies, would undoubtedly be the face of this romantic, ruthless battle. The first armed uprising of the Naxals in India was indeed imbued with this spirit of adventure, romance, even innocence. Suman, who wears his empathy with the Maoists on his sleeve, was referring to this spirit of romance. All that Suman's quote suggests is that taking up arms against the CPI-M's armed militia was a fleeting, impulsive thought that crossed both Suman's and Mamata's mind in a situation that seemed to have become desperate, tinged with a sense of poetry rather than a desire for programmatic political violence.

Did Mamata plot with the Maoists to subvert the law and order situation in West Bengal in order to dislodge the already tottering Left Front government? Highly unlikely. Was there a convergence of the Maoists' and Trinamool's political objectives? To an extent, yes. All three movements—Singur, Nandigram and Lalgarh—were born outside the pale of formal party structures. Their diversity accommodated groups that may not have been in agreement about strategies of protest and resistance.

The discussion of West Bengal's culture of competitive violence shared by armed workers belonging to both CPI-M and the Trinamool Congress camps should not be conflated to the thesis that the Trinamool Congress was working in perfect tandem with the Maoists to realize their political project. The questions that seem relevant are: Do the Trinamool workers on the ground, and across districts, keep their distance from the Maoists? Or do the Trinamool workers and Maoists exchange arms and fortify each other against the Left Front government?

Interestingly, Mamata too has accused the CPI-M of being in league with the Maoists, a somewhat fantastic charge. The dominance of violence in West Bengal's political culture makes it possible that the Trinamool fought the comrades with arms. The escalation of violence in the aftermath of CPI-M's crushing defeat in 2009 and the Trinamool Congress's recent electoral victories are just a couple of the many corroborating evidences. In a culture where knives and bullets are wielded freely to claim political ground, to square up with political opposition in day-to-day life, the Trinamool need not enter into a pact with the Maoists. Arms are easily available and acquired here.

The CPI-M did not get much electoral mileage out of its Mamata–Maoist nexus campaign. But it did try hard. After every incident of violence in the state, after every public meeting the Trinamool chief attended, after every speech she delivered, the accusations would resurface. On 9 August 2010, addressing a public meeting in the heart of Lalgarh, Mamata said the manner in which Azad, a top Maoist leader, had been killed was 'not right'. She demanded that the government investigate the incident. All hell broke loose when the media picked up this speech and the CPI-M pointed to the statement as further vindication of its theories. Interestingly, four months later, in January 2011, the Supreme Court asked the Central government and the state administration in Andhra Pradesh to explain how exactly Azad had died in the Adilabad forests of Andhra Pradesh, making it clear that the case was far from a simple 'anti-terrorist' action by the administration.

As West Bengal's assembly elections approached, the CPI-M accelerated the thrust of this campaign. Chief Minister Buddhadeb Bhattacharjee responded to Home Minister

P. Chidambaram's request for disbanding the CPI-M's armed militias (Harmad Vahini) with his own list of camps testifying to the 'Trinamool–Maoist alliance'. In October 2010, sabotage by suspected Maoists led to the horrifying Gyaneshwari Express accident, claiming 150 lives. In her first reaction to the incident, Mamata pointed a finger at the CPI-M, insinuating that the ruling party could have plotted the sabotage to defame her. The CPI-M retaliated, coming down like a ton of bricks on the 'absentee' railway minister, accusing her of 'hobnobbing' with the Maoists. Umakanta Mahato, a prime Maoist suspect in the Gyaneshwari sabotage, was later killed by the security forces in a gun battle.

As usual, the truth probably lies somewhere in between. It is highly unlikely that Mamata Banerjee would have jeopardized her political prospects by endorsing the brand of politics practised by the Maoists. Electoral democracy is not the way that the Maoists engage with the political class. Even if Mamata, as Opposition leader, had hoped to befriend them in pursuit of the classic 'my enemy's enemy is my friend' approach, the political cost of swinging deals with the Maoists would have been far too dear. She had waited a long time to reach where she is now.

Acquiring arms however has become as common to West Bengal's political culture as abarodh or blockades on streets, highways and railway tracks on every issue of importance. But how convincing is the CPI-M's continued attribution of all the ills that have befallen it to the handiwork of Mamata and the Maoists? Not very, for the people did not bite the bait. Mamata won the corporation elections hands down after the horrifying Gyaneshwari Express derailment—the continuation of a political trend that began in the 2008 panchayat elections and culminated in the 2011 assembly elections. The Lalgarh movement ought not to be remembered as a symbol of a Mamata–Maoist alliance, but for what it actually represented: yet another section of Bengali society, long forgotten by the government, rising in protest against the order of things, demanding basic needs that it had long been deprived of.

5

Taking Over the Cultural Space

The militant upsurges in the villages and tribal regions of West Bengal saw a massive attrition of the Left Front's popular base. This coincided with its loss of traditional support among Muslims in both rural and urban areas. The Left's loss was Mamata's gain, an opportunity to renew her engagement with the Muslim community. She could try and make up for teaming up with the BJP in the NDA government and for not dumping the alliance even after the Gujarat pogrom.

The bulk of the peasants involved in the 2006 Nandigram agitation were Muslims who, in the course of the movement, gravitated towards the Trinamool. According to Kabir Suman, Siddiqullah Chowdhury of the People's Democratic Conference of India (PDCI), who played a crucial role in the Nandigram movement—even before Mamata arrived on the scene—threw in his lot with Mamata. This was a hallmark of the Singur and Nandigram movements, where individuals like Siddiqullah drifted towards the Trinamool chief. It is another matter altogether that many of these organizations and individuals later moved away from the Trinamool Congress, accusing it of high-handed behaviour.

Rizwanur, Taslima and Mamata

In 2007, the mysterious death of thirty-year-old graphic designer Rizwanur Rehman, who was married to the daughter of Marwari industrialist Ashok Todi, presented Mamata with a fresh opportunity to reach out to the Muslim constituency. She demanded a Central Bureau of Investigation (CBI) inquiry into the murky collusion between Ashok Todi—who had vehemently opposed the inter-religious, inter-class marriage of his daughter Priyanka—and a section of top police officers, including Kolkata's police commissioner Prasun Mukherjee. As Kolkata exploded in outrage, Mamata visited Rizwanur's family. She demanded the removal of senior police officials known to have been pressuring Rizwanur to end the marriage. Mamata met Governor Gopalkrishna Gandhi, urging him to ensure a CBI inquiry into the matter.

The Rizwanur case was indicative of larger problems in the state. The Rajinder Sachar Committee Report of 2006 had bred disenchantment among the state's Muslim community, impelling the shift away from the Left. The report had some pretty stark figures on how Muslims were faring under the secular Left Front government. In a state where they constituted 25.25 per cent of the total population, Muslims held only 4.2 per cent of government jobs. More than 3,000 villages with predominantly Muslim population had no medical facilities, and more than 1,000 villages no educational institutions. At a public rally on Kolkata's Mayo Road on the eve of the assembly elections,

Mamata invited the author of the report, former Delhi High Court chief justice Rajinder Sachar, to West Bengal. She told the gathering that included villagers from North 24 Parganas, South 24 Parganas and East Medinipur—all districts with a large Muslim population—that she would seek suggestions from Justice Sachar on how to improve the condition of Muslims. The deliberate reference to the report and its author was aimed at increasing the discomfiture of the ruling CPI-M.

When it came to the vote bank or electoral calculations however, Mamata was as ruthless as any politician. There is no better indication of this than her stance (or the lack of it) on Bangladeshi author Taslima Nasreen, which indicates that like with most political leaders, electoral calculations tend to gain an upper hand over matters of ethics and principles. Mamata remained silent in two critical situations, both having at their heart the controversial Bangladeshi writer who made Kolkata her home after being forced to leave her country by Muslim fundamentalists. The controversial writer was attacked by Majlis-e-Ittehadul Muslimeen (MIM) MLAs in Hyderabad at a book release function. Mamata kept mum. Then again, when the Left Front government bundled the author out of the state overnight after a section of Muslims staged violent protests on Kolkata's streets, the Trinamool chief had nothing to say. On 21 November 2007, protesters gathered under the umbrella of the All India Minority Forum and fanned out across the city, armed with cold drink bottles, handmade missiles, inflammable glue and brickbats. Their immediate grievances: forcible land acquisition in Singur, the conspiracy around Rizwanur's death and Taslima Nasreen's presence in Kolkata. The police and the Rapid Action Force (RAF) kept vigil, but did not use water cannons or rubber bullets. The situation was on the boil, and the army was called in later in the afternoon. As dusk fell, the protesters dispersed into Kolkata's alleys and warrens.

The government decided that the author's continued presence in Kolkata might trigger a riot. But the protesters were not merely demanding the expulsion of Taslima; they were also agitating against the Nandigram and Rizwanur episodes.

When the media asked Mamata what she thought of Taslima's peremptory ouster, she had no comment to offer. Mamata said that the Central government was already looking into the matter. Ironically, there were voices among the Muslim community raised in support of Taslima and in condemnation of the demand for her ouster. After all, she had been living in the city for three years without being a risk to its law and order situation. The All India Minority Forum, responsible for the street violence, was a fringe group. It may have been an error of judgement on Mamata's part to conclude that support for Taslima would alienate her minority voters.

But it was this fear of losing the support of a section of Muslim voters that spurred the CPI-M to ban Taslima's book, *Dwikhandita*, and then summarily evict her from the state. Mamata—for all her claims of being an alternative face in West Bengal politics—did not rise above vote-bank pressures. Mamata's irrational impulsiveness, her irascible temperament, emotional reaction, her instinctive solidarity with the underdog—none of this was in evidence. On display instead was the shrewd calculation of a politician, her willingness to factor realpolitik into her calculations.

Mamata's close associate Mahasweta Devi, on the other hand, spoke up for the banished writer. On the third anniversary of

Nasreen's departure, Kolkata's literary luminary sought her return to the city. 'I also ask those in favour of change to come forward,' she said. 'All kinds of criminals can stay in the city, but Taslima cannot. Her only fault is that she is a writer. [...] The way Taslima Nasreen was forced to leave the city is one of the reasons why CPI-M is being asked to leave West Bengal. The notice for her departure was an unpardonable offence.'[1]

This may be one of the reasons why Mamata's silence on the episode was not, however, seen as being an anti-Taslima stance. Soon after the 2011 assembly election results, Taslima was quoted by newspapers saying she hoped to return to Kolkata now that the CPI-M was no longer in power. Taslima's statement is also an indication of how the cultural scene of West Bengal is now shifting towards the Trinamool.

Culture in the Trinamool Congress

Our quest to understand the many contradictions that make Mamata may be well served by an insight that singer-songwiter-activist Kabir Suman can provide. An independent Left-wing artiste, he made the transition to being a Trinamool Congress MP (though, later, he fell out with Mamata and reclaimed his autonomous status). 'I first saw her on the grounds of Uluberia in an agitation of Kanoria workers,' he writes in his book. The year was 1994. 'She was a political leader; I was a musician and an activist. She was on the podium that day. I was outside, having made it clear to the leaders of the movement that I would not share the podium with any political leader.'[2] This independent activist, straining against all authority, had no way of knowing that, a decade down the line, he would contest elections from the prestigious Jadavpur constituency, and that at the request of the very leader with whom he had refused to share a dais. Or that he would end up winning and entering Parliament.

But his intimacy with active politics ended soon after. Today, he is a pariah in the circles that once pushed him into taking the electoral plunge, cashing in on his fame, popularity and image as a Left cultural icon. Post retirement, he penned the controversial *Nishaaner Naam Tapasi Malik*—published in 2010, and now in its fourth edition—a political tract of his experience in the movement with Mamata Banerjee.

In some ways, Kabir Suman represents that quintessential Leftist who made a transition from disliking Mamata Banerjee to liking, even admiring, her. This is Suman's description of Mamata at the Kanoria meeting: 'I had heard that she was incredibly popular among the people, though I had never met her in person. Honestly, I never had much interest in politicians; not then, not now.' But, he points out there was a disjuncture between the Left's strong aversion to Mamata and her popularity among the masses: 'I noticed that the Leftists did not like her even though the general people, some of them I personally knew, did indeed like her very much. Some of the Leftists known to me would even make derogatory comments about her.'[3]

For Kabir Suman, the key to Mamata's popularity was her aggressive combat against the CPI-M. He admired her for this. Suman speaks of how, since 1992, the CPI-M had been harassing him in various ways. 'I will not lie—I liked this person's dogged fight against the CPI-M. However, I found her sometimes to be too emotional, if not theatrical. In politics, though, performance is indeed a major factor. Many prominent politicians are also prominent actors.'[4] But Singur and later Nandigram, in which he was Mamata's fellow traveller, put paid to these reservations. By 2009, he had come to believe that he must firmly support the Trinamool against the ruling CPI-M.

Suman was not alone. Many artistes and intellectuals who shared his initial reluctance to endorse Mamata changed their minds after the intense struggles in Singur and Nandigram. They acknowledged her as the only viable force capable of beating the Left Front, and joined her camp. In fact, like Suman, artist Suvaprasanna and theatre personalities Saonli Mitra and Bratya Basu also extended their endorsement to joining the Trinamool in various capacities. In the general elections in 2009, Mamata fielded several celebrity candidates, including Suman and prominent film personalities like Shatabdi Roy and Tapas Pal. And, like Suman, many of these new supporters were sympathetic to what we might broadly call 'Left politics'.

One of them, theatre director Arpita Ghosh, had this to say when I met her in Kolkata: 'I am personally a Leftist. I was born in a "Left period", and grew up during the Left regime. In Scottish Church College, while studying, I engaged with Naxal student politics. In our college days, we always slighted right-wing people, never cared much for them. During the 1980s, it was impossible for me to believe in and align with any force other than the Left. But we have been watching now for a long time the steady deviation in Left politics.'

Ghosh links Mamata's ascendancy very clearly to the Singur agitation: 'That is where the Mamata Banerjee magic started. As leader of the Opposition, she handled the movement very well. Though a Left movement in its essence, it was not led by Left parties. On the contrary, the CPI-M expected to bully the protesters into giving up land.' Ghosh, like Kabir Suman and many others, occupies a significant place in the narrative of Mamata's transition from a politician they would have earlier dismissed as rightist to one who has gained widespread legitimacy among Left-leaning cultural icons.

This is not surprising when you consider that Ghosh is representative of a large number of artistes who have found themselves at the receiving end of CPI-M's Stalinist practices. Arpita ran into serious trouble with the CPI-M over the staging of *Poshu Khamar*, a play based on George Orwell's *Animal Farm*. The CPI-M stopped the play from being performed not only when it was riding high on power, but even as recently as on the eve of the 2011 assembly elections, when it seemed to have lost the battle. Arpita and many other cultural personalities who have journeyed through this turbulent period have been able to reclaim their political space and the right to have a say in politics.

Ghosh remembers watching the relentless police violence in Singur on television. 'You cannot disbelieve your own eyes. I had to speak. Nothing else mattered. Pancham Baidik, our theatre group, can proudly claim that this was the room where the movement among artistes started. Two activists from Singur came here and told us about their fight. A couple of days before that, Tapasi Malik had been murdered. On 10 December, [the Bengali poet] Joy Goswami penned a poem which we sent to Buddha with a letter wanting to know what exactly was happening in Singur. The audience at our shows signed our petition [as did] a host of other artistes. After a lengthy silence, Buddhababu sent us a booklet printed by Alimuddin Street [CPI-M headquarters]! Many of us felt we had to now take the fight to the streets. Mamata Banerjee was then on fast at Dharamtala. We did not know her personally. A proposal came to us to share the podium with her, but we decided to fight independently. Our stand was that Mamata Banerjee should continue her agitation but we would do our bit independently.' It was another three years before Ghosh met Mamata Banerjee at an interaction organized by Suvaprasanna.

To Bratya Basu, director of theatre group Bratyajan, and now minister of education in the West Bengal cabinet, Mamata Banerjee is a torch-bearer of what he referred to as the 'sahajiya' school of Indian philosophy as against the westernized intellectual Brahmo tradition in Bengal. 'What we see now is an assertion of this sahajiya culture reflected in the quotations cited by Mamata from Ramakrishna, Sarada and Vivekananda. This aspect of Bengal's life is reflected in the Mangal Kavya, in the literature of Bharatchandra. Mamata Banerjee is the face of this change,' Bratya said in an interview with me.

The decisive and active role of intellectuals in West Bengal politics is not really a novel phenomenon. What is novel is the shift of Left-leaning artistes and intellectuals to the political forces they have traditionally been opposed to. It may not be an exaggeration to say that the intellectuals' shift to the Trinamool may in part have been prompted by the search for an autonomous cultural space.

Grass-roots organizer and social planner V. Ramaswamy told me why he made the transition: 'I have been a non-establishment Left person from the time I entered public activism in 1984. However, during elections, especially with regard to the Congress as it was then, I used to vote for the Left Front in state and parliamentary elections. I think from the 1990s I used to destroy my vote. I was profoundly opposed to the CPI-M and the Left Front government of West Bengal.' And then Singur-Nandigram imploded. Ramaswamy participated in the Nandigram movement. 'But it was in mid-2009, when I travelled through some districts of West Bengal in connection with a study for the World Bank, that my thinking underwent real change. I saw for myself, first-hand, what the TMC had achieved in remote areas where it did not have a traditional base. They had reached out to fine people, the grass-roots leadership was impressive to my eyes, people of India should be proud of. The results of the Lok Sabha elections in 2009 had just come out—I voted TMC in it—and my respect for Mamata grew.'

Some of the artistes aligned with the Trinamool were appointed heads of various railways and cultural committees. Critics argue that the 'converted' have forfeited their status as 'intellectuals' by giving up the autonomy, the academic and artistic independence, which defines any prominent cultural action. Instead, the accusation runs that these pro-change artistes have allowed themselves to be shackled to a political party, drawing salaries from party-sponsored departments and committees.

The debate over intellectuals and autonomy is likely to turn more metallic in the time to come. Now that the state's politics has turned a corner, the intellectuals and cultural personalities now tied to the Trinamool may have to contend with a new set of conflicts. For decades now, the CPI-M too has advertised its closeness to intellectuals, artists and bhadralok. Cultural personalities ranging from Ritwik Ghatak and Mrinal Sen to Sunil Gangopadhyay and Utpal Dutt have all been identified as closely allied to the politics of the Marxists in power. The charges levelled against many fellow travellers of the Trinamool today might have something to do with the desperation that the Left feels at losing its last bastion: culture.

Bratya Basu's play *Ruddhasangeet* (The Song that Was Stifled), staged on the eve of the 2009 elections, portrays the agony and the humiliation suffered by artistes like Ritwik Ghatak, Utpal Dutt and Salil Chowdhury at the hands of the Communist Party. The play captures the intrinsic conflict between artistes yearning to express their creative, imaginative instincts and the party's desperate moves to exercise Stalinist control over them. They chafed at the regimented construction of culture as nothing but a tool for party propaganda and the muzzling of contrarian artistic expression.

Ruddhasangeet, running to packed houses at Kolkata's Academy of Fine Arts, has at its heart the iconic Rabindrasangeet singer Debabrata Biswas, his involvement with the Gananatya Sangha, his parting of ways with the Communist Party, and his differences with Viswa-Bharati University's music board. But the play is situated in an era when a whole range of artistes in West Bengal, from film-maker Ritwik Ghatak and musician Hemango Biswas, to poet Subhash Mukhopadhyay and theatre director Sambhu Mitra among others, were closely associated with the Communist Party. The analogy with the CPI-M's rampant censorship of plays or songs critical of its politics was too sharp to miss. The playwright, like many others in his fraternity, had been subjected to CPI-M's cultural coercion when the performance of his play *Winkle-Twinkle* had been stopped. First performed on the eve of the 2009 Lok Sabha elections, the play ran to a packed house. Known for his proximity to Mamata, Bratya attracted the criticism that he was using his play to popularize the Trinamool Congress. Many theatre groups he had been close to ostracized him after his association with Mamata began with Singur and Nandigram. One of these groups even publicly disowned him at a press conference.

An artiste's relationship with authority and political parties is necessarily conflicted. If Bratya has any apprehensions of such a conflict arising in his engagement with Mamata's politics and culture, he does not share them. 'Rarely would you meet a more civilized, polite person. And after seeing her come through so many tough situations, yes, I have indeed become her fan,' he declares. Bratya says, nonetheless, that his alignment with the Trinamool does not mean that he will be in the bondage of that party the rest of his life. 'If Mamata Banerjee does something that I cannot accept, I will change my stand.' Whether he will be able to make good his promise remains to be seen. He is now the minister of higher education in West Bengal, having won the assembly elections in 2011 from the Dum Dum constituency as a Trinamool candidate.

Whether the new converts achieve their aspirations under Mamata and her leadership of West Bengal, of course, remains to be seen. Arpita Ghosh too claims that her support to the Trinamool Congress cannot be taken as granted for all times. 'Today I am a Trinamooli. If tomorrow Mamata Banerjee does something I vehemently disagree with, I will stop supporting her… We supported the Left parties but when they deviated we took a different stand,' she points out. It is her view that the IPTA-like resurgence of a cultural movement in West Bengal, the likes of which have not made an appearance for three decades or more, will leave a long-term impact. 'Whoever comes to power will have to take this new resurgence, the proactive intellectuals and artistes into account. We cannot be taken for granted. Nor can we be treated as pushovers or captive loyalists.'

Avant-Garde and Kitsch

As the assembly elections neared, the situation was tinged with a touch of both comedy and theatre. Buddhadeb Bhattacharjee and Mamata Banerjee—the two 'warriors'—were engaged in a contest as much political as cultural. Gopalkrishna Gandhi once said, 'In how many places can one find a bibliophile Chief Minister who also writes poetry with sensitivity, and an Opposition leader who sings and paints with feeling?'[5] We do not know whether the governor's comment was prompted by dead earnestness or a touch of humour, but it does point to the importance of culture in the political landscape of Bengal.

Buddhadeb is known to take great pride in his cultural sensibilities. He is conscious of being the nephew of Sukanta Bhattacharya, the radical poet who died young. And he was a particular favourite among members of the film community. Over the years, Buddhadeb has picked up the coveted tag of a 'cultured' chief minister. He has penned plays. His book of poems, *Chena Phooler Gondho* (The Fragrance of Familiar Flowers), was written for the stage. An admirer of authors like Gabriel Garcia Marquez and Vladimir Mayakovsky, he translated their works into Bengali. On the eve of the 2006 elections, his last political triumph, immersed in hectic campaigning, the chief minister told reporters 'the literary self of mine has gone on leave for the moment'.[6] As West Bengal's culture minister, he was instrumental in setting up Nandan, a state-run film theatre, which shows mainstream as well as niche avant-garde cinema and has evolved into a cultural hub of sorts in Kolkata.

Two months ahead of the crucial assembly elections in 2011, Pulitzer winner Richard Ford inaugurated the Kolkata Book Fair, which for the first time had 'America' as its theme. Buddhadeb boasted about Kolkata's close relationship with American authors and poets. The works of Walt Whitman, William Faulkner, Jack London, Edgar Allan Poe, E.E. Cummings and Ezra Pound were, he said, immensely popular among the city's readers. On more than one occasion, playwright Arthur Miller's works have been translated and his plays staged. Kolkata held a special charm for poet Allen Ginsberg who visited the city in the mid-twentieth century. Underlying these assertions by the chief minister was the Left's confidence that this progressive, radical history was its own.

If Mamata felt cheated of the exclusive silver screen company her adversary kept, her chance to make up the deficit came in November 2010. At the request of Information and Broadcasting Minister Ambika Soni, she inaugurated the 41st International Film Festival in Goa. Standing in her plain white cotton sari and rubber flip-flops before the film community, she said that she had no idea what someone like her was doing in a world of glamour. With her characteristic down-to-earth wit and her mix of Bengali-English, she told members of the audience that their 'life isn't a joke: they can't eat even if they are hungry! Always dieting!'[7] Her unpretentious speech was an instant hit with the gathering. Assuring them that she would take up the problems of the film industry with Finance Minister Pranab Mukherjee, Mamata said, 'Talking to Pranab-da is easy. From Mamata to Pranab-da, I assure you there will be no dadagiri.'[8] While campaigning in the 2011 assembly elections, Mamata promised she would transform the Satyajit Ray Film and Television Institute into a world-class film production studio—that is, if the Trinamool came to power.

The battle for Writers' Buildings has also been a battle for cultural spaces. Not so surprisingly, Mamata and her arch rival are united in their passion for Rabindrasangeet and Gurudev Tagore. Buddhadeb is not known to sing, but Mamata is, and at one time used to frequently break into Rabindrasangeet. A simple search on YouTube shows some performative examples. 'She actually has a rather nice voice. I used to tell her that she should practise music more and perhaps become a singer rather than a politician,' Krishna Bose told me during a conversation. Mamata paints, and writes prose and verse; she has more than a dozen books to her credit. If you walk into her office at Kalighat, you are likely to find her armed with tubes of paint and painting material. Often it is an outlet for her anger.

Sujato Bhadra describes an incident when he had gone to meet Mamata in the wake of the controversy that had erupted in the media over Kabir Suman's insistence that they publicly support the Maoists. This was in the aftermath of the Lalgarh movement's descent into violence and the eruption of a national debate on Maoism. His book, which was supposed to be a confession of his links with Maoists, had not yet hit the stands. The Trinamool had begun to rein Suman in and the spat between him and Mamata had become a high talking point in Kolkata. 'The Kabir Suman–Trinamool tension was peaking and some of us sought an appointment with Mamata before the matter went out of hand. She immediately gave us time. When we entered her office, Mamata was painting. All of us were nervous about how she would react to our suggestion that for the time being she should not say anything negative about Suman to the media. As I started speaking, I could see clearly that Mamata was getting furious though trying not to show it. She was squeezing the tube of paint in her hands really hard, oodles of paint was oozing out!' On another occasion, a senior Trinamool leader told me, 'Just the other day, we were at this programme when Didi was sketching. This is her way of taking the tension off.'

On the other hand, if you catch Mamata in a good mood, she may gift you with one of her paintings or a poem she has written. Reporters who have been invited to dine at her place recall her singing Rabindrasangeet after a sumptuous Bengali dinner and her gifts of books or sketches. But then for all of this to happen, Didi has to be in the right mood. No wonder people are terrified of her mood swings and of being in the line of fire.

While both Buddhadeb and Mamata lay claim to the title of cultural aficionado, there is a vast gulf separating the content of their cultural consciousness. Their 'language' and cultural, political and philosophical moorings are all different—the Left's high culture posited against the Trinamool's tawdry aesthetics. The Left has always believed, and still does, that they are intellectually superior to the 'unenlightened' political classes, particularly their homespun adversary Mamata Banerjee. This superiority has been historically grounded in a context where the top artistes have been firmly aligned with the Left.

In the post-Tagore era, most literary giants were aligned with the Left or with a broader radical politics. 'The great majority of Bengali poets and fiction writers, with Manik Bandyopadhyay and Bishnu Dey in the lead, have helped build an imposing edifice of Left tradition in literature. A Congress-minded novelist, Tarashankar Bandyopadhyay, parted company with the Left fairly early in his career, but the tales he narrated of decadent feudalism and evolving new class alignments bear the signature of Left convictions. A later literary celebrity, Samaresh Basu, changed camps, but could not quite unlearn his early grooming in Communist Party cells,' observes Ashok Mitra.[9] Even earlier, before World War II, Buddhadeb Bose had worked closely with the anti-fascist writers and artists. Mitra points out that even a staunch critic of Stalinism, like eminent poet Sudhindranath Dutta, had co-founded *Parichaya*, a journal that engaged with aspects of Marxist theory and practice, introducing the people of West Bengal to the debates within Marxism and Left politics. Sambhu Mitra, Utpal Dutt and Ajitesh Bandyopadhyay, three thespians who towered over the world of theatre, were all members of the IPTA. Top musicians, from Rabindrasangeet singers to singers of folk songs and radical music, were either members of the Communist Party or sympathetic to its ideology. Given this history, it is sheer hypocrisy to single out pro-Mamata intellectuals as deviating from the virtues of artistic autonomy. While the desire for a cultural politics that is not subservient to the state must be foregrounded, the analysis must also recognize that culture has never really been 'free' of politics—in any sense of the term.

The 'superior' quality of their culture, the Left would like to believe, has stemmed from their ideology and politics, their philosophy. Class struggle, oppression, exploitation, liberation and revolution have been the soul and substance of every form of art produced by Leftists and those close to them. Straying from these themes often automatically attracted the labels of 'degenerate bourgeois' or 'petit bourgeois culture'. The Left has had a compulsive need to convey what it believes to be its 'higher philosophy' through art and literature.

Here is what Ritwik Ghatak had to say on the subject: 'From Goethe to Sukanta, life has moved on. [...] The oppressed masses have wrenched from History its scientific world view through the agency of Karl Marx.'[10] The director then goes on to say that these two developments have 'redefined the content of the utterance of the poet and the method of art'.[11] Ghatak quotes a couple of verses from Shakespeare's *Hamlet* to fortify the philosophy of the oppressed. To him Shakespeare *was* Hamlet: 'He took up the great sufferings and agonies and unbearable pains of his fellow men, oppressed men, and nurtured them,' Ghatak said.[12]

Although there are, no doubt, much greater complexities that exist in the cultural productions of Left-leaning intellectuals, the basic distinction between the Left and the Trinamool does still sustain itself to some extent. Regardless of Ghatak's brilliance as a film-maker, the simplified *political* understanding of culture I am sketching here does, by and large, capture the CPI-M's view of things. There is, however, another argument that remains: that the Communist Party's interpretation of works by their 'chosen' artists doesn't always hold good; that the films of Ghatak are, for example, more complicated than the CPI-M might like.

In spite of this qualifier, the point I am making here is that the fundamental cultural and political language of the Left is far removed from the Trinamool Congress chief's homespun religious, spiritual themes of popular communication. In fact, the cultural 'pastiche' that Mamata offers stands in stark contrast to the Left's great cultural lineage, from home-grown heroes to Walt Whitman and Allen Ginsberg. In the first chapter of this book, I have tried to present briefly the essence of the philosophy of Ramakrishna Paramahansa, undoubtedly among the most prominent influences on Mamata's life. If the Left's cultural idiom has been shaped by the philosophy of class struggle, the Mamata brand of culture is heavily reliant on Rabindranath, religious leaders like Ramakrishna Paramahansa and Vivekananda, and spiritual texts like the Gita. This is something we have to understand to comprehend what is happening today.

Mamata says she is a believer in 'humanism'. Unlike the Marxists, who swear by the doctrine of internationalism (though that did not deter the CPI-M from labelling the forces of resistance at Nandigram and Singur as 'outsiders'), Mamata had her gaze squarely and unwaveringly fixed on the limited space occupied by West Bengal. 'After all, I am from Bengal—"Bengal's soil, Bengal's atmosphere, Bengal's produce" [from a Tagore song] are my valuable heritages. [...] While standing beside the stranded tourists from Bengal after the devastating earthquake in Uttarkashi, I had wanted to say only one thing: "I am one of you, let me be known by this identity."'[13] Mamata is aggressive about expressing her identity as a Bengali, as a leader from Bengal, and this identity is inseparably woven into her political agenda and with her finally realized ambition to wrest power from the ruling CPI-M. Mamata addresses her audiences through basic parables—the words of Ramakrishna, Vivekananda, the Gita and the Upanishads—which are at complete odds with the Marxian language of the CPI-M.

From 2006 onwards, Mamata began to appropriate the political rhetoric of the Left. She announced in Nandigram that her party was the new heir to the 1947 Tebhaga movement, led by peasants and the Communist Party, demanding peasants be given two-thirds of the share of crops tilled by them.[14] Songs of the IPTA began to resonate at her rallies. On 8 January 2010, at the foundation-stone-laying ceremony of a hospital, Mamata Banerjee sang *We Shall Overcome*. At a public meeting on 21 July 2009, the mother of Nurul Islam, a martyr of the 1966 hunger march, was seen sitting on the podium. 'This is visible political appropriation of a representational reserve,' suggests Moinak Biswas.[15]

Mamata's form of politics is new, and it proceeds along the two axes I identified in the first chapter: on the one hand, she 'borrows' the cultural-political idiom of Left radicalism, and, on the other, she infuses into this doses of a post-bhadralok politics. This new form blends religious and spiritual aphorisms with the rhetoric of land struggles, human rights, justice and development for the poor. So the language she deploys to communicate politics is not just peppered with Left imagery, but also carries a liberal dose of religious and spiritual content. Even as she whips up passion over Tebhaga, Mamata invokes Ramakrishna and Sarada, Vivekananda, the Puranas and the Gita. Mamata Banerjee is deeply religious and, in her distinctive style, she brings this flavour to the meetings she addresses, the literature she authors, and the general culture she creates around her. She is a regular visitor to the popular Belur Math—something that increases her appeal among large sections of the common people. Almost every household in Kolkata has pictures of Ramakrishna and Sarada, and Mamata knows this. Straddling the two opposite ends of a cultural and political spectrum—simplistically and incorrectly referred to as the Left and the Right—she mixes idioms effectively, catching the imagination of people, at least for now when her popularity is at an all-time high.

To understand the power of her mix-and-match ideology, you would have to attend a meeting she is addressing. On 7 February 2011, flanked by a bevy of her party's political heavyweights, Central ministers, railway ministry officials, artistes, authors and musicians, Mamata announced the inauguration of a new Metro Railway line at a large public meeting in the heart of Kolkata's Salt Lake area. Most of her functions, small and large, are usually preceded by musical soirees and the Salt Lake meeting was no exception. Kolkata's famous rock music group Bhoomi and the Metro Cultural Group sang Rabindrasangeet and Salil Chowdhury's songs, interspersed with rhythmic strains of rock music. In the midst of the singing, Mamata arrived, a diminutive figure, almost invisible among officials and the Railway Protection Force personnel surrounding her. She seemed familiar with the Bhoomi crew, chatting casually with them on the podium and asking them to continue with their singing. She was to honour the author Sanjib Chattopadhyay and the singer Dwijen Mukhopadhyay. Chattopadhyay delivered a brilliant address, punctuated by acidic wit, spiritual philosophy and political innuendo. Though he was not in the 'Mamata camp', Chattopadhyay made it clear that her's was the side he was on for the time being. Invoking the image of 'Durga' and 'Shakti', he said Mamata would extricate Bengal from disarray.

Mamata's own speech was packed with references to Ramakrishna, Sarada, Vivekananda, Saraswati (with Saraswati Puja around the corner), and Hindu textual-religious philosophy, with an accent on work and duty. 'We should take every opportunity to work. Our lives are ephemeral. Nobody lives here permanently. Every second, minute, hour, month, year is important. We think we should work only before elections. You have to utilize the moment at hand.' She then moved on to 'humanism', a recurrent theme in her books too: 'Ramakrishna said some call mother maa, some amma, some mother, but the essential humanism underlying all three is the same. Vivekananda used to say "never say no". If you have failed a thousand times, try once more. We have heard the same message sometimes in Netaji's words, sometimes in Ramakrishna's, sometimes in Nazrul's, and sometimes in Rabindranath's. We want that Bengal's young girls and boys should never say no.'

This package of religion and philosophy, jumbled though it may be, carries a less than oblique reference to the non-performance of the thirty-four-year-old Left Front government. The harping on 'no' is a not-so-indirect reference to the CPI-M and its trade union CITU's famous 'chalbe na' politics. Banerjee's insistence on 'performance' through references to the Gita is also clearly a dig at West Bengal's culture of non-performance.

To the delight of her audience, Mamata announced her intention to name a Metro station after Paramananda, guru of Bharat Sevasram Sangha. But she also picked Sukanta, the emblematic radical Left poet, and said she would name a station in his honour too. The Marxists think these antics ridiculous, but the people at large do not seem to mind. Some grumbled about the frantic naming and renaming of stations, but not about the religious/spiritual coating on politics. After all, people in West Bengal are known to practise their religious and political faiths side by side, making place for Marx as well as Ramakrishna. But what they are not used to is hearing these invocations from a political pulpit.

The transition in the political culture of West Bengal, evident in the language deployed by the leaders of the CPI-M and Trinamool, is also reflected in the decor of their respective party offices. If you walk into Alimuddin Street, the sombre, imposing portraits of Marx, Engels, Lenin and Stalin greet you. Inside the Trinamool Congress Bhawan, a big painting of Kali hangs above a door at the entrance of a party functionary's office on the first floor. These visual motifs are subtle indications of the kind of changes occurring in the political landscape of Bengal today.

One aspect of this change finds expression in Mamata's efforts to revive memories of Bengal's celebrities. Naming metro stations after them is just one aspect. On the evening of 12 February 2011, at a star-studded function in south Kolkata, the Trinamool-run Kolkata Municipal Corporation announced a committee to revive Uttam Mancha, a hall built more than a decade ago in honour of the cine star Uttam Kumar. Mamata announced that the dusty hall, forgotten and uncared for, will be turned into a spanking cultural centre for staging plays. As is normal at Trinamool functions, well-known musicians, old and young, regaled the gathering with Rabindrasangeet. Neighbourhood residents came down from their high-rise apartments to listen to the music and to Mamata. 'We will revive West Bengal's past cultural glory, identifying stages like Uttam Mancha, which are lying in neglect. We will find ways to use them as cultural centres,' Mamata claimed. She also spoke of a Kolkata Municipal Corporation project to accord heritage status to the house of one of the legends of Rabindrasangeet, the late Suchitra Mitra, and to Rabitirtha, her music school.

The revival of the lost glory of West Bengal is a prominent theme in Mamata's speeches—whether through exhortations to inculcate a culture of work, promises to bring in industries, provide jobs and stem the exodus of youth, or by reminding people of how the Left Front government had ignored their matinee heart-throb Uttam Kumar. At a time when West Bengal has little going for it, these assurances of putting the state back on the rails can seem attractive enough.

It is almost impossible to separate Rabindrasangeet from Mamata's daily transaction of political business. Some may complain that the flavour is too dramatic, too emotional. But given Rabindrasangeet's unique status in people's lives, rather than talk during campaigning in the Kolkata Municipal Corporation elections in 2010, Mamata was heard reciting '*Jirna puratan jak bheshe jak*' (let the old and worn be washed away), lines from Tagore's famous song '*Bandh bhenge dao*' (Smash the dam). She greeted the Election Commission's announcement of West Bengal's poll schedule for the assembly elections of 2011 with '*Tumi nabo nabo rupe esho prane*' (May you come into my life in ever new forms). She told the media that the elections, being held in the month of Baishakh, coincide with the Bengali New Year and will herald a fresh beginning. Her style and content of campaigning, peppered with religion, prose, verse and songs certainly seem to be working. This is evident when Bratya Basu says he is drawn towards Mamata's political aesthetics without making any reference to her painting, music or poetry. 'She is a creative person, whose politics will reflect that,' he says. He contrasts the Left's 'westernized' cultural philosophy with Mamata's indigenous, grass-roots aesthetics.

Not all in the intellectual and artistic fraternity—including many who have firmly shut the door on the CPI-M—are pleased with the new 'converts' and their proximity to Mamata and her party. They do not believe this will usher in an alternative politics. Some of the questions thrown up in this debate are: Can intellectuals hold on to their independence in spite of a complete identification with a political party? Is the need for change at this moment greater than autonomy?

In an opinion piece in *Anandabazar Patrika*, Asim Chatterjee, one of the original Naxal leaders, wrote: 'The pro-changers are eager to label the intellectuals who are not ready to do the bidding of political parties as "frauds, betrayers and opportunists". There is only one problem. Intellectuals no longer remain intellectuals if their allegiance to a political party is a necessary precondition to active intervention in politics. They then become party workers.'[16] At the heart of the debate as expressed by Chatterjee is also the yearning for an alternative content and form of politics. There is apprehension that the new rulers in the Trinamool may not break the cycle of partisanship and patronage. Besides, there is no denying that, among the new celebrity votaries of Mamata Banerjee, there are some opportunists who have been inexorably drawn by the possibility of imminent power. Even Trinamool leaders can identify the rank opportunists among their new devotees. But opportunism comes with the terrain; the more the Trinamool succeeds, the more its ranks will swell with people of all kinds.

Sujato Bhadra believes that, regardless of reservations and doubts, Mamata is the only face of hope and of an alternative: 'She has captured the popular mood of the people, winning over even those who were opposed to her.' Sujato, speaking to me before the elections, said Mamata was the only force that could reckon with the CPI-M and defeat them. The truth is that Bengal's intellectuals are split down the middle. It may be fair to say that a substantive section of them are driven by heartfelt, sincere passion for change, while others are driven by a love for power, and others still may have a bit of both.

The majority of those who held on to the CPI-M were partly motivated by their commitment to the party and their belief in its politics, partly by the attractiveness of power, and maybe even sheer habit. What this historical narrative shows is that the charges levelled by the Left against Trinamool sympathizers cannot be adequately understood without taking into account the Left's own sense of 'loss' over culture as a domain that was uniquely its own. In turn, the cultural flux in the state right now, as I argued in the first chapter, must be placed within the broader context of the disintegration of bhadralok culture—a culture that the CPI-M, in spite of itself, is now fully identified with.

6

The Performance of Politics

In the lead-up to the 2011 assembly elections, the high enthusiasm and keen anticipation of 'paribartan' drew some unusual people to the Trinamool Congress. Sabeer Bhatia, Hotmail founder and an entrepreneur, was one of those who teamed up with the party to help it strengthen its cyber communication platform. 'People of West Bengal are working for change and I am here to share some of my ideas for better communication,' said Bhatia.[1] Hariharan Sriram and Mansha Tandon from Kolkata's Indian Institute of Management took up internships with the Trinamool Congress. 'After thirty-three years of Left rule, the Trinamool Congress is now in the forefront to bring about a possible change. It will be amazing to watch it from inside the system,' Mansha said when contacted by the media.[2] The interns worked online, communicating with people till results were declared on 13 May.

The media and Mamata's theatrical politics are complementary elements, and this is an aspect we must examine to understand her role as a 'performer' on the stage of West Bengal—and to unravel the person that is Mamata Banerjee.

The spectacle of politics has always had an organic connection with the aesthetics of theatre and the dramatic elements of performance. This connection is only heightened in an era of fast-paced cyber communication and tele-visually manufactured images. Spontaneously and instinctually, politicians across the spectrum have morphed into performers, stringing out witty one-liners and acerbic, wry comments—staging thespian moments captured by the 'third eye' that hardly ever seems to avert its gaze from its subject. Some are more skilful than others in staging a performance and the idiom of theatre is more often than not symptomatic of the culture of politics today. Boris Groys writes: 'The problem is not art's incapacity to become truly political. The problem is that today's political sphere has already become aestheticized. When art becomes political, it is forced to make the unpleasant discovery that politics has already become art, that politics has already situated itself in the aesthetic field.'[3]

Some performer-artist politicians play on their personal traumas and dark misgivings, while others choose the medium of comedy, sometimes mocking themselves, at other times evoking ribald laughter. Mamata falls into the first category, and Lalu Prasad is an accomplished practitioner of comedy. Distinct as their performative styles may be, both leaders have tapped into a popular non-elite consciousness. During the 1980s and 1990s, Mamata's performances were marked by shrillness and a high melodramatic quality. They were often compared to, and seemed to be inspired by the popular Bengali folk theatre form of jatra. Underlining the script was her volatile personality, always awash with runaway emotions.

Far too many of Mamata's reckless, unconventional and theatrical acts of venting her disaffection played out before she reached the heights she now has. The Oxford dictionary defines histrionics as a 'personality disorder marked by shallow volatile emotions and attention-seeking behaviour'. Whether Mamata was deliberately 'seeking attention' or was simply unable to rein in her transient, explosive emotions could well be a matter of debate.

In sharp contrast to her is the persona of Lalu Prasad, who skilfully prepared his comedic scenes, using his rustic lineage, his sense of comic timing and his Bihari-intonation-inflected English. It was a potent combination. Posing before cameras in his banian, he effortlessly entertained his audiences: villagers, the well-heeled urbane middle classes and, of course, the media. His earthy, coarse humour never failed to bring them comical, light-hearted relief. Some argued that he trivialized the politics of the underclass by using his own persona as an object of spectacle.

Mamata's theatrics was imbued with a quality as morbid as Lalu's was playful. Her performances seemed to be driven by subterranean emotions—dark anger, sometimes at her own party, the Congress, which she could not trust, but most often at the verbal and physical attacks launched by her adversaries in the ruling CPI-M. Her morose performances went hand-in-hand with the dark prose she wrote, a testimony to her fears and anxieties. Tormented by the thought of being stabbed in the back by her warring party colleagues, Mamata was driven to periodic frenzied outbursts. Like Lalu, Mamata was a great performer, but she on her stage—that of West Bengal's volatile politics—was the tragic actor. And she was good. Mamata could drum up a frenzied pitch of hysteria, like the time she had her supporters crying and shouting, trying to persuade her to file her nomination papers for an election.

In the early days of her career, Mamata had no light-hearted moments, at least not before an audience. Lalu—who set himself up as the jester, using his hair, his attire, his syntax, to bring light-hearted cheer to his audience—may have appeared to be playful, even foolish, but that too was subversive in its own way. Just as Mamata chipped away at the last reserves of an elite bhadralok culture, Lalu brought the underclasses to Delhi and thrust them in the midst of India's premier institutions of governance. But instead of arriving with a sense of awe, he turned politics into spectacle. Once the apple of the eye of the masses in Bihar, Lalu's hair, cropped to the scalp in short spikes, became a trendsetter. Local barbers started giving their customers a 'Lalu-style' haircut. And the artful master of playful gimmicks used the political stage to 'entertain' rather than execute an act of tragedy.

Sedate in her appearance with her hair severely pulled back into a bun and a carelessly worn sari, Mamata was and continues to be a perfect counterfoil to an image like Lalu's. The CPI-M's constant dismissal of her jatra style of histrionic politics, even during the assembly elections of 2011, is a testimony to just how cut off the Marxists were from the popular idiom of tragic-melodramatic politics. The slogan 'Maa, Maati, Manush' itself feeds into and gains strength from that popular idiom. On the other hand Mamata—cosying up to industrialists, splurging on modern electronic campaigns, winning over IIM graduates and individuals like Sabeer Bhatia—has also crafted an alternative image as a serious politician, one who is more concerned about being with the people and setting West Bengal on the right path than living a life of luxury as chief minister. So, as she emerged as a serious contender to the throne of West Bengal, Mamata's image had to undergo a makeover.

In all of this, the media plays an all-important role. Groys argues that 'in our time, every politician, sports hero, terrorist, or movie star generates a large number of images because the media automatically covers their activities. [...] Every important political figure and event is immediately registered, represented, described, depicted, narrated, and interpreted by the media.' Occurrences in West Bengal for the past five years have epitomized this mediatization of politics: from Singur and Nandigram to the images of Buddhadeb Bhattacharjee travelling in a jeep as Mamata walks on foot, media images have played a significant part in crafting how we react to both sides. And it seems that it is Mamata Banerjee—melodrama queen, yet restrained politician—who has understood the art of existing in a mediatized world far better than her communist rivals.

As the cry for paribartan reverberated through West Bengal, anxieties gave way to hope and a keen sense of anticipation. The two-decade-long wait seemed to have been worth it as Mamata entered the combat zone and made an aggressive bid for Writers' Buildings. And this time, the people of her state, the leitmotif of her politics, rallied around her in tens of thousands, signalling the end of an era in the political narrative of West Bengal.

7

Preparing for the Transition

In the run-up to the momentous 2011 assembly elections, Mamata Banerjee was as much in the grip of her treadmill as she was of Rabindrasangeet. As the chief minister's chair beckoned from Writers' Buildings, Mamata readied for a gruelling campaign in the heat and dust of West Bengal. With the strong whiff of impending success, this assembly election promised to be like none other. In 2001, her slogan 'Ebaar noi to never' (now or never) had haunted Mamata after her party's dismal performance. A decade later, having broken through the once unbreachable Left barricade, she was now more confident than ever before. The years of forlorn waiting, of holding out empty threats to the Marxists, were now behind her. All she had to do now, Mamata's colleagues told her, was to keep physically fit and mentally cool; the treadmill was meant to take care of her physical fitness, while the music would soothe Didi's nerves and neutralize her public rages. This was utterly necessary, at least for the next few months.

Mamata has an eclectic taste in music, listening to all sorts of sounds: the jagged rhythm and bordering-on-bizarre lyrics of Bengali rock jostle with soulful Rabindrasangeet and high-spirited Nazrulgeeti. Her runaway temper, her colleagues vouch, is now well under control.

Today, Mamata is no less tormented than her well-wishers are by the thought that if her mercurial temper got the better of her one day, it would wreak havoc on her now-respectable reputation. In the past, the inexorable pull of her impulses had driven her to actions that unceremoniously landed her in the midst of political wilderness. Rather than risk her new-found credibility, Mamata has expanded her range of stress busters. Besides working out on the treadmill, she practises yoga and takes brisk walks. These anti-stress activities must have stood her in good stead when she undertook the hugely publicized padayatra in the lead-up to the polls, attracting massive numbers of people everywhere she went. Images of her energetic campaign on foot made for a stark contrast with Chief Minister Buddhadeb Bhattacharjee's jeep yatra, waving at people from the confines of his vehicle. The dramatic contrast between the two images seemed to function as a revealing metaphor for the widespread acceptance of Mamata Banerjee as a popular leader of the state, and Buddhadeb as representing a party thoroughly disconnected from the masses.

But self-discipline did not always work for Mamata even during this crucial period. The wicked temptation to shout her opponents down did rear its head once in a while, like the time she was presenting the railway budget in the Lok Sabha on 26 February 2011. Raising a din and demanding more trains, Bihar's contingent of MPs refused to allow her to speak. Some would say that Mamata was getting a dose of her own medicine: recall her throwing her shawl at Ram Vilas Paswan, railway minister, more than ten years ago. No match for Mamata's careless flamboyance, the Bihar MPs could only vigorously exercise their vocal chords as high as their lung-power would allow. Through her spectacles Mamata glared, reprimanded them and tried not to fly into a tizzy. The MPs kept the pitch high, straining her patience. 'If you do not listen I will cut,' she said. 'Please listen, first to last you listen then you shout. Please be ready...' Then: 'Dekho bhai, mere ko pronunciation kharab ho jaiga chillane se, mere ko ahista ahista bolne do (My diction will be spoilt if you shout, let me speak slowly)...'

With her gentle reprimands falling on deaf ears, Mamata finally gave in to her old craving. 'Don't shout ... I cannot satisfy everyone,' she screamed at the Bihar brigade. Her irate language, a patois of English, Hindi and Urdu, with splintered sentences hanging in between, words hammered and broken to keep perfect pace with her nimble thoughts, was like her Duronto Express—non-stop once she began. Although such displays of frustration did her no favours as far as the national media was concerned, this method of speaking is something Mamata has made her own.

She has managed to turn her frailties, especially the imperfections of her syntax, into a perfect 'dialect' of communication, into a popular idiom-defying nomenclature. Her flawed semantics, offensive perhaps to language purists and certainly inviting the contempt of the privileged, instantaneously connect her with her audience. If the result induces the effects of a comedy show, it is purely unintentional. Unlike Lalu, Mamata has no predilection for provoking instant hilarity. Bihar's greatest political showman used to revel in throwing around droll one-liners; his unfamiliarity with the English language was put to comical effect as he entertained the media, generating mirth all around. Mamata, on the other hand, does not really care if her flawed recitation of Urdu couplets or the lyrics of Lata Mangehskar's '*Mere vatan ke logon*' provokes a derisory laugh or two. She knows that, back home, she can hold an audience captive with her anarchist use of language. Her voters don't complain; and that is what matters.

Didi Comes of Age

Mamata's struggle in the recent past has been to expand the ambit of her supporters, to gain a more expansive legitimacy. To understand that struggle, the question we must ask is: to what extent did she manage to overcome the barriers of class, language and culture?

On 18 February 2011 Mamata shared a podium with a host of Oxbridge speakers at a debate sponsored by the *Telegraph*. They were addressing a 5,000-strong audience in Kolkata's Netaji Indoor Stadium. The motion of the debate: 'India will be better run if politicians were left out of the government.' Apart from Mamata Banerjee, the other panellists included journalist Swapan Dasgupta, academics Dipankar Gupta and Ramachandra Guha, cricketer Rahul Dravid, media personality Suhel Seth, and Congress politician Salman Khurshid, all of whom spoke a polished tongue and a sophisticated rhetoric. Mamata opposed the motion in her typical fractured syntax, careening between English and Hindi, as well as pitching a bit of Bengali.

'I want to see pollution-free politics. If there is no pollution, there are so many good people who will come into politics. They may not be from Harvard or Cambridge, but they are from the grass roots. They may not know batting and bowling but they know fielding,' Mamata argued. Taking a pot shot at the panellists for chiding politicians, yet not risking joining politics themselves, Mamata said, 'There are some bad people, some good people. You can identify them. But there are some goody-goody people who cannot be identified.' Turning to Swapan Dasgupta and Suhel Seth, she asked them to join active politics. She said politicians are as integral to the government and the country, as 'balls to cricket', 'CEOs to industry', 'headlines to newspapers' and 'breaking news to channels'.

If the 'Letters to the Editor' in the next day's edition of the *Telegraph* were any indication, the 'chief-minister-in-waiting' clearly carried the evening, emerging a winner in the popularity contest. Here are three samples of that 'vote':

> Speakers for the motion looked lost even before Mamata Banerjee rose to speak. Her unadorned but 'positive' approach was enough to vanquish the opposing arguments. It was expected that Banerjee would receive the loudest cheers from the audience, but one could see that the applause was well-deserved after she finished speaking. When her colleague, Salman Khurshid, described her as the 'chief-minister-in-waiting', she received the compliment with a poised smile… From her speech, it was clear that she has matured as a politician, and has acquired the acuity and resilience of a mass leader.
>
> —Adhip Kumar Bose

> The *Telegraph* National Debate will be remembered because of its speakers, who were fabulous. But Mamata Banerjee stole the show despite not being a seasoned debater ('Mamata vs. rest and one winner', 19 February). She drew a clear distinction between 'bad' politicians and 'good' ones, and strengthened her case by

stating that though there is corruption in the form of betting in cricket, all cricketers cannot be seen as corrupt because of this. Her choice of expressions sometimes lacked finesse, but she enthralled the audience with her spontaneity and directness.

—A.S. Mehta

All those who watched Banerjee speak would agree that she has matured a lot, abandoning her earlier hysterics to become a capable, new-age politician, and perhaps the 'chief-minister-in-waiting'.

—Anirvan Sengupta

In the prelude to the assembly elections, much of the debate around Mamata—on roads, in drawing rooms, at tea stalls, in local trains—centred around her personality, her transformation, if at all, from a hot-headed, militant, impulsive activist to a stable, thoughtful chief ministerial candidate. A lot was at stake, not only for the aspirant for the chair, but for West Bengal. Barring the CPI-M and its faithful, hardly any voices were heard arguing for a continuation of the Left regime. The doubt, fears, hopes and aspirations in Bengal revolved around Mamata Banerjee and the transition she was on the brink of making, personally as well as for the state.

But how radical was the eventual transformation?

Here is economist Abhirup Sarkar's point of view: 'Probably, at one point Mamata Banerjee was naive, sentimental from an emotional point of view. Even today she is very emotional; her driving force is emotions. But now she does think with her head. She has definitely matured as a political leader as is evident from the political decisions she is currently taking.'

One of the indicators of her newly acquired maturity was the way she handled the post of railway minister from 2009, the importance she lent to her post. Soon after the Election Commission announced West Bengal's poll schedule, a confident Mamata told reporters, 'I will not contest the assembly polls. I do not want to confine myself to one constituency. All the 294 constituencies are mine.' If the Trinamool wins, Mamata will have six months to get elected from any constituency. 'I can always fight from a constituency within six months and get elected,' she said to the media, even as the CPI-M tried, oddly, to argue that not contesting somehow revealed a 'weakness' in her. Mamata was keen to retain charge of the railway ministry as long as rules permitted, having realized its potential in terms of the weight it could add to her personal stature and to the development of West Bengal. The Trinamool chief had indeed come a long way since the time when, in a huff, she threw away the key post during the NDA regime. By 2011, the developmental potential of the ministry had sunk in well and truly.

A former senior bureaucrat of the railway ministry told me during an interview, 'This is a ministry of political patronage. Unlike any other ministry, this one has tremendous political potential and a direct impact on political and electoral dividends. From Madhav Rao Scindia, Jaffer Sharief and Lalu Prasad to Mamata Banerjee, everyone has extracted political mileage.' But it was perhaps for the first time that the railway ministry found a head who practised austerity with such exacting severity. The former bureaucrat remembers an incident from Mamata's first stint as railway minister, then in the Vajpayee government. A special secretary in the ministry greeted Mamata with a bouquet of flowers. Rather than being pleased, the minister started interrogating him about the source of payment. Had he bought the delightful bunch of flowers with the ministry's money or paid from his own pocket? On being told that the officer had spent his own money, Mamata asked him what it cost, and then proceeded to deliver a neat sermon on profligacy, and how her own saris cost about the same as that bouquet.

Mamata's second tenure as railway minister, beginning in 2009, was plagued by controversy about the 'absentee minister' who was far too preoccupied with messy politics back home to do any justice to her cabinet job. Often missing in Parliament, the railway minister shuttled between the Centre and West Bengal, where her emotional and political interests truly converged. The Gyaneshwari train accident was the most prominent of the many incidents that occurred during her tenure and led to heavy criticism from her political opposition—from the BJP to the CPI-M. In the aftermath of the Gyaneshwari mishap, there was a feeling among many that Mamata had jumped the gun in speaking immediately of 'conspiracy' and 'sabotage', pointing to her opponents in West Bengal. This was, her critics said, the conduct of a Central minister caught up in her own political battles and willing to sacrifice the bigger picture.

In August 2010, there were news reports that further bolstered these allegations, particularly the revelation that Mamata's absence from Delhi forced officials to fly to Kolkata with documents that needed her attention. This process—of five officials travelling between Delhi and Kolkata—apparently cost the exchequer over ₹11 lakh. Besides the fact that this strengthened allegations of Mamata's disregard for her responsibilities at the national level, it also undercut her image as an austere politician. But these allegations did not unduly disturb Mamata, nor did her Bengali electorate seem to care. At some level, Mamata recognized that she *was* making a choice between Delhi and Kolkata. The

Central ministry was useful to Mamata insofar as it reinforced her position in the state and allowed her to plan a route for the economic recovery of West Bengal. If her political life had been characterized by the single-minded mission to throw the Left Front out of Bengal, it came as little surprise that Central ministry berths and the perks of political life in Delhi were not of much concern to her.

Whatever vexed signals she sends out on other matters, Mamata has not the slightest ambivalence where her home state is concerned. No wonder then that in the midst of the ruckus during the presentation of the railway budget in 2011, Mamata thumped the desk and shouted, 'Yes, I am proud of my state!'

In her autobiography, Mamata writes, 'My well-wishers (do they really wish for my well-being?) have on many occasions said that I have resigned too often. I had resigned from the cabinet because I wanted to devote more time to Bengal. [...] I am willing to risk my life to do whatever is necessary to ensure that Bengal's honour is in no way hurt. The people of Bengal can repose their faith in me over this matter without any fear. It is this trust that I have over the people which is my support for the future. I will not allow my Motherland's honour to be laid to the dust. The soil of Bengal, the water of Bengal are our invaluable assets. Bengal is still our pride and our hope. It was Bengal which had in the past lit up the beacon in the spheres of civilization, culture, creativity, etc. Bengal's valour and bravery had no parallel. When I think of this I feel emotionally thrilled.'[1]

Through all the criticism and allegations she had to face, Mamata never shifted her sight from Writers' Buildings. She pressed the railway ministry into the service of Bengal, to benefit its people and, of course, the Trinamool Congress. The minister primarily functioned from her Kalighat residence. Bureaucrats, hugging their files, moved in and out of the Trinamool office. On the eve of the railway budget, with the assembly elections round the corner, the minister worked from home, the bureaucrats in attendance. She also went on a binge, announcing more and more railway projects, naming and renaming countless metro stations after eminent personalities. Not everybody was taken in; critics questioned the viability of her schemes. The new names she had given metro stations seemed to be an inconvenience for passengers, leaving them clueless about the stations' actual locations. Even within Mamata's party, some people were complaining. 'Names of stations should indicate the area, the locality, which help commuters,' cribbed a former Congress, now Trinamool Congress, leader. Mamata's long list of names included luminaries like Mahatma Gandhi, Bankimchandra Chattopadhyay, Saratchandra Chattopadhaya, Prafulla Chandra Roy, Rajendra Prasad, Anukul Thakur, Mangal Pandey, Uttam Kumar, Sukanta…

Still, Mamata's politics of renaming was not simply to extract political mileage from the names of cultural icons. The roots of her renaming craze lie in the cultural flux that I discussed in the previous chapters. With the erosion of the Left's traditional stranglehold on culture as the backdrop, much of what Mamata was doing could be understood as an attempt to 'capture' an essential part of her identity: non-elitist, religious and rooted in popular culture. And the critics of Mamata's project are being disingenuous when they imply that her renaming project is something new. In the recent past, the Left Front too had used renaming as a political strategy. While Mamata renamed stations, the Left Front's renaming activities transformed the entire landscape of the city. The road many of us grew up calling Lower Circular Road one day became Acharya Jagadish Chandra Bose Road; Theatre Road became Shakespeare Sarani; Harrington Road was christened Ho Chi Minh Sarani; Park Street—one of the most iconic locations in the city—was renamed Mother Teresa Sarani; Camac Street transformed to Abanindranath Tagore Sarani; and Free School Street was given the name of Mirza Ghalib. As this list (also Mamata's) makes clear, renaming is a complicated act, intrinsically connected to the assertion of culture as a domain of politics. It also shows the need that political parties feel to establish a cultural-political 'lineage' within which their own image can be crafted.

With Mamata formulating expansive and expensive schemes and programmes, critics wondered where the finances would come from and how long it would take to operationalize them. But people in Bengal had reason to smile. The expansion of the Metro Railway greatly improved connectivity, linking suburbs, strengthening the communication network. Mamata promised the city a seamless railway linkage, connecting the commuters to both local trains and the metro. If the proposal materializes, the commuter, through a series of interfaces, will be able to get off a train and board the metro with the same ticket. Seven new metro surveys announced thirty-four additional trips for Kolkata. 'I propose the development of integrated suburban railway networks, bringing together suburban and Metro Railway and other rail infrastructure under a single system which will provide faster, efficient, affordable and comfortable transportation,' Mamata said in her budget speech in 2011.

The Big Push Theory

The biggest charm that the railway ministry held for Mamata was probably its potential to act as a catalyst, to be the 'big push' in West Bengal's economy and development. The departure of the Left Front government will not magically lead to economic resurrection. The challenges ahead of the Trinamool are daunting, what with an economy that is tottering on its last legs. Mamata's magic slogan, calling for 'change', resonated so strongly and among so many because they were fed up of the never-ending status quo. These people now want to see early the signs of change, or at least the will of the next regime to overhaul the present malfunctioning system.

A few months before the assembly elections, Abhirup Sarkar told me that the 'railway sector can provide the "big push" needed to get the economy up on its feet. Ancillary units as well as infrastructure can be built around this sector which will bring to the state private sector investment. At present, West Bengal's poor infrastructure is a serious deterrent to private investment.'

'Big push' is an old economic theory that gained currency in the 1950s. The Soviet economy, during its period of growth, debated whether some sectors should play a lead role and, through the linkages built around them, push the development of other sectors. In England, the 'big push' came from the textile sector; in Japan, from textiles and light engineering, which paved the way for a flourishing automobiles sector.

Mamata, it would appear, has rolled out her own 'big push' policies. In a two-pronged strategy, she has leveraged the railway ministry as an agent of change not only in West Bengal, but also at an all-India level. For instance, the 2011 railway budget has proposed setting up a track-machine industry in Uluberia, a metro coach factory near Singur in West Bengal, and a railway industrial park in Nandigram, the latter two aimed at scotching apprehensions of Mamata's perceived 'anti-industry' stand. Outside West Bengal, the minister proposed a coach factory in Kolar through public–private partnership, and a factory in Jammu and Kashmir to build bridges for railway projects. In addition, the first coach from the new rail factory at Rae Bareli was set to roll out within three months of her speech. If the 'big push' strategy works, it will route West Bengal's much-needed industrialization through the railway sector; at the same time, the strategy will enhance Mamata's image, as well as that of her party, at the national level.

One of the serious challenges confronting the Trinamool, however, is the intractable conflict over land acquisition. It is to Singur and Nandigram that Mamata owes her political and electoral turnaround; any reversal in her stand could cost her dearly. Having categorically ruled out land seizure through coercion, Mamata has maintained that land will only be acquired through peaceful means, and only if people voluntarily agree to give it up. To further complicate the tangle, the CPI-M has advertised publicly its intent to play tit-for-tat politics; in other words, Mamata is likely to run into belligerent opposition from the CPI-M and its mass organizations. The CPI-M may not have played the role of the Opposition for a while in Bengal, but it is a game the party is very good at.

Mamata got a taste of the politics of backlash when she had to cancel a ₹85-crore coach factory project at Sankrail in Howrah district in 2010. The CPI-M mounted a strident protest against the setting up of any industrial establishment in the area, alleging that Mamata would very likely not keep to her word to provide employment for those displaced by the project. The railway minister decided not to initiate work at Sankrail in the face of these protests, and said instead that she would return when there was no opposition. The railway minister hinted at the challenges before her in her budget speech: 'I wanted to set up a coach factory at Singur but land has not been made available by the state government. However, several landowners have volunteered to sell their land directly to the railways. In order to fulfil this commitment, I propose to set up a metro coach factory on the land purchased from willing sellers at Singur, adjacent to the Polba block.'

The war of attrition has only begun to warm up in Bengal. The CPI-M will try its very best to muddy the image of the new government. Perhaps the most bitterly, maybe even viciously, fought terrain will be industrialization and development. The CPI-M's likely strategy will be to square up with the Trinamool for Singur and Nandigram. Abhirup Sarkar, nonetheless, remains optimistic. 'If the ordinary people want a project, nobody can stop it—whether it is Haldia or Sankrail. If free competition kicks in, ending the CPI-M's terrible partisan approach, industrialization will truly begin,' the economist argues. He says that, apart from the use of violence, it was this favouritism that sealed the fate of the Nano in Singur. 'People knew the contract for a construction wall at the factory site would be given to the party's own people. There would be no fair competition. Those loyal to the Opposition or neutral would have no chance of staking a claim. This was a major disincentive.' The government that succeeds the CPI-M will need an imaginative, non-partisan approach to industrialization specifically, and economic growth more generally.

West Bengal's severely fractious environment and the legitimacy that the politics of vendetta finds there are big hurdles that Mamata must cross. To make good on her promise of 'change', Mamata will need to uproot the deeply entrenched sources of partisan politics. She will also have to tread lightly on the terrain of land and industry. Earlier, the railway minister had proposed a land bank, mapping the land owned by her ministry. The idea was to survey the resources and make them available to the industrialists. A proposal was on the anvil to institute a committee of business houses to work out a rational business plan expediting work on the Eastern Corridor. The 1,806-kilometre-long Eastern Corridor will extend from Dankuni to Ludhiana and pass through several mining and industrial towns. Dankuni will serve as a major hub, which Mamata hopes will provide jobs to local people. Clearly, her strategy was to use the land available with the railway ministry to minimize the scope for conflict.

This seems to be the way she plans to deal with land acquisition in the near future too. A few months before the assembly elections, at a public meeting in Haldia, Mamata announced the construction of a new port at Sagar by reclaiming 2,000 acres of land using silt after dredging. No fresh land acquisition was required in that instance either. Attending the meeting was also MP and Union Minister for Shipping Mukul Roy to lend credibility to the project. Mamata also announced her proposal for a wagon manufacturing factory at Nandigram—again, the project did not require any forcible acquisition of land. 'The Burn Standard Company had taken land here. It is on this land that we will build the factory. The railways have already acquired this land,' Mamata told the meeting.

West Bengal's Nitish Kumar?

In 2010, Abhirup Sarkar went to Patna to attend a large conference organized by the London School of Economics and Oxford University. Its theme essentially analysed the changing context of Bihar and the road ahead. 'At that conference, the question repeatedly nagging me was what was it that Nitish Kumar could achieve that we [West Bengal] could not; a second related question was, what went wrong despite Buddhababu winning such a landslide victory in 2006? There was such euphoria around him; the entire national and international media were buzzing. In fact, the Nitish hype was less than that of Buddhababu's,' he said. Nitish Kumar was the chief minister who shifted, practically overnight, Bihar's governance paradigm, ushering in a political culture far removed from extortions, abductions and general lawlessness?

Here is Mamata's account in 2005 of Bihar under Nitish Kumar: 'Last 23 November, I attended the swearing-in ceremony of the new government in Patna at the government's invitation. I witnessed the heartfelt emotions of the people of that state. I saw how their verdict toppled a fifteen-year-old government. The swearing-in was held in Patna's Gandhi Maidan. Deeply moved, I saw several lakhs of people arrive, not in cars or forcibly mobilized, but on foot. They wanted to witness the unveiling of a new future. Gandhi Maidan was bursting at its seams. Truly the people expressed their endorsement even before the new government had begun to function. I thought the wind of paribartan is blowing across Bihar. Will this wind of change also touch Bengal?'[2] The question then is: does Mamata have the wherewithal to be the Nitish Kumar of Bengal?

Mamata's job is likely to be tougher than his, though. In some spheres, Bengal's economy and its concomitant culture fare worse than Lalu's Bihar. Ironically, the CPI-M's organized party structure, lauded for its centralized command and its dense capillary of party organizations, had spawned an unusual system of party-linked corruption. Under Lalu, ruled by a dishevelled Rashtriya Janata Dal, Bihar practised the 'ordinary' kind of corruption: all-pervasive, sometimes outside of the control of the party in power, at other times institutionally fed. But the case of West Bengal is qualitatively different—here, the austere lifestyle that the communist leaders propagate ensures that corruption does not take the virulent financial forms it does elsewhere: not many party leaders accrue huge amounts of money as they govern. But the party has presided over major corruption for decades, aided by its strong statewide organizational structure. Sarkar explains how this perplexing phenomenon works: 'In West Bengal, corruption is organized. In other states, what happens is, you make scattered payments to get your work done. The CPI-M is so organized, all you have to do is make a single-window payment, a 'bribe' to the party. No need to make payments elsewhere. Pay the party half the amount of what you need to pay as tax. Your work is done. Only an organized party can do this. In other states, it is cheaper to pay tax, otherwise you end up having to grease the palms of a lot of people. In West Bengal, on the other hand, it is cheaper to pay the party. For instance, instead of VAT, small traders can pay the CPI-M.'

According to Sarkar, the striking thing about Bengal's economy is its pathetically low tax collection, ranking the state among the lowest, if not *the* lowest, among all Indian states in revenue collection. 'The CPI-M has cost the state exchequer a huge loss of revenue. The government, as a consequence, has run up a steep debt,' he says. As a result, the Left Front government's finance minister drastically slashed government expenditure, meeting only basic requirements, like payment of salaries, interest, dearness allowance, pension, etc. The government stopped investing in capital expenditure, roads, basic infrastructure, and this kept the investors out. Even the states that were once clubbed under the tag 'BIMARU', have accumulated capital. But Bengal—despite its decades of rule by the CPI-M, and thus having a political stability that is rare in India—has not.

If West Bengal has to turn around, Mamata will have to deal with these complex and daunting challenges on a war footing. No doubt her party too is afflicted with corruption; even when not in power in the state, the Trinamool was jostling with CPI-M workers to get their 'commissions and cuts' from real estate lobbies and promoters. The nexus that corroded the vitals of the CPI-M has already got a grip on Mamata's party. However, Sarkar says, without the CPI-M's organizational structure, the Trinamool's corruption won't be very different from that of other parties and governments in the country.

The character and quality of the Trinamool Congress do not always inspire confidence. Some drew cold comfort from Mamata's own impeccable financial honesty and, paradoxically, her 'dictatorship' over party colleagues and workers. 'Mamata Banerjee gets livid if anybody, even her family members, use her name to further their personal interests,' said human rights activist Sujato Bhadra. But in West Bengal's political arena, personal financial honesty and a frugal lifestyle are not unique to Mamata. Top CPI-M leaders have a reputation for financial integrity and ostentation-free modest lifestyles. Buddhadeb Bhattacharjee, for instance, lived as a tenant in his two-room 59B, Palm Avenue flat for thirty years, even as chief minister. He had no property in Kolkata and became the owner of his 700-square-foot Palm Avenue flat only in 2011.

Nonetheless, there is something impressive about Mamata's scrupulous honesty in a country where a shadow of sordidness hangs over the political class—scams tumble out day and night, ministers are handcuffed, money siphoned off to foreign banks, public servants stockpile wealth. The unhealthy influence of large corporations and kingpin industrialists over political parties, and the largesse handed out to the kith and kin of political leaders have scarred the political establishment. Mamata's parent party, the Congress, has hardly been a stickler for financial rectitude. Right now, it stands accused of spawning several 'mother of all scams', one after another—from the Commonwealth Games to the 2G spectrum. When it comes to moral high ground, the difference between Mamata and the Congress could not have been starker.

Those who have worked with Mamata speak of her painstaking efforts to save the money of the departments she heads, as well as her warm and polite interactions with the staff, regardless of their position. Her colleagues tell the story of when, as minister for youth and sports affairs, Mamata had gone to the Maldives to attend a meeting of the Commonwealth ministers. On her return, she returned her entertainment allowance. Since ministers are not in the habit of returning foreign exchange, Mamata's gesture, rather than bringing on smiles, caused a bit of worry. The officials wondered how they should redeposit the money. Mamata advised them to convert the dollars into rupees to solve the problem. After quitting as minister in the Narasimha Rao government, Mamata donated her salary to the National Sports Welfare Fund. Though her resignation, submitted on 25 November 1992, was accepted two months later, on 18 January, Mamata did not avail of the entitlements due to her in the interim period.

As the Trinamool proudly shows off its leader's financial integrity, the Congress—its alliance partner once again in Bengal—is drowning in a swamp of scams (from the embezzlement of funds in the 2010 Commonwealth Games to a colossal loss of revenue in the irregular 2G spectrum allocation in 2008, to a myriad other administrative and political troubles, from the controversy brewing over the proposed nuclear plant in Jaitapur to the party's non-committal stand vis-à-vis farmers and tribals over projects like POSCO's steel plant in Orissa).

Even as the public reacted to this endless barrage of accusations and exposés, the Trinamool advertised some novel methods of revenue collection to fund its political campaign. Barely a fortnight before the first phase of the 2011 assembly elections, Mamata exhibited her paintings, where ninety-five out of the 200 works on display were for sale. The reason: her party's lack of funds. The exhibition was also meant to set Mamata and the Trinamool apart from other political parties whose election campaigns were known to be funded by one industrial group or the other. Organized by the Trinamool Congress's mouthpiece, *Jago Bangla*, and curated by artist and Mamata supporter Suvaprasanna, the three-day solo exhibition was open for twenty-four hours a day. This was not the first time that Mamata has used her paintings to raise money. The first exhibition was held in 2006, and the second was organized at Ashutosh Centenary Hall two years later. The latter exhibition earned her a sum of ₹11 lakh, which she donated to the victims of police attacks in Nandigram.

Mamata has zealously (even overzealously) guarded her image as the austere, honest politician. Her Spartan lifestyle, humble lodgings, Gandhian attire, proletarian speech and fearless courage have crafted an image that's rare among politicians. In her autobiography, *Struggle for Existence*, Mamata says she stopped wearing silk saris after entering active politics. She narrates how Prafulla Sen, former chief minister of Bengal, had presented her a silk saree following her victory from the Jadavpur constituency in 1984. 'He gave me a silk saree and told Khuku-di to ask me to wear the saree and show him. He was elder to me, so it was not possible for me to disobey him. Yet, he did not know that I had stopped wearing silk saree after entering active politics. I just could not make him understand. Then I sought Khuku-di's help. I told her, "Khuku-di, please explain to him I shall wear it later on."'[3]

The contrast of this image with the stereotype of the greedy Indian politician impresses and pleases her voters. As she said in the *Telegraph* debate, not all politicians can be tarred with the same brush. A distinction between the 'good' and the 'bad' politician is imperative to believing that something worthwhile can come of the political process. At present, the Trinamool leader is firmly ensconced with the 'good' in her fraternity. In the corridors of Parliament, potential third-front leaders, loath to abandon hopes of a non-Congress, non-BJP alternative, have tentatively identified Mamata as a long-distance runner. They believe that her clean image and her now elevated status as chief minister can make her a rallying figure around whom disparate regional parties can coalesce. One of the stories Trinamool leaders are fond of narrating is of then prime minister Atal Bihari Vajpayee's visit to Mamata's Kalighat residence. After spending some time in Mamata's home and meeting her mother, the prime minister is believed to have said that he would have had far less problems running the country had there been more honest politicians like Mamata.

Dictator or Democrat?

If there's one conclusion that we draw from this discussion, it is this: to speak of the Trinamool Congress, basically, is to speak of Mamata Banerjee. What is her relationship to her party? Is the party only 'incidental' to her political goals? Mamata *is* her party and the Trinamool *is* Mamata. She is accountable to no one in her party, and none of her party colleagues dare to question, let alone challenge, Mamata's decisions.

Few, even among her diehard fans, would deny the overwhelming streak of dictatorship that underlies Mamata's personality. 'Her organizational grip is supreme,' says Bhadra. 'You need a dictator like Mamata in her party,' says Arpita Ghosh. 'I am a theatre director and I am a dictator,' says Bratya Basu. Leaders in the Trinamool Congress are 'terrified' of Mamata's spiky outspokenness, her sudden—often inexplicable—bursts of anger. They fear her merciless, sometimes public, tongue-lashings. The smart ones avoid appearing before Mamata when she is with outsiders or addressing the media. What if she suddenly flies off the handle, leaving them with red faces in front of the media? They had seen it happen to others.

Here's a hilarious instance of that fear in action. During the 2011 budget session, actor-turned-politician Tapas Pal, dressed entirely in black, entered Mamata's office in Parliament. Smiling at him warmly, the minister recited: 'Baa baa black sheep have you any wool/Yes sir, yes sir Tapas's bag full!' The author of several books of poems, Mamata is known to frequently break into rhyme. Tapas was trapped in a nervous dilemma: was his party president complimenting him or was she shooting off a sarcastic barb? In the end, unwilling to risk hazarding a guess, the MP left the room, hurriedly and in silence.

Mamata is quick to axe colleagues hankering after privilege. She also does not take kindly to being challenged by her colleagues. One remembers, for example, her sacking Ranjit Panja and Sudip Bandyopadhyay. Over the years, Mamata's politics of sacrifice has mellowed to accommodate the compulsions of realpolitik. But even today, she is impatient with her MPs eyeing cabinet berths. Didi's mood swings keep everyone on tenterhooks. If in a good mood, she will chat with and indulge you; if not, she will blanch you with her caustic, intemperate remonstrance. Those tracking Mamata's career say she is capable of being vengeful and spiteful. Others point out that, though given to acting in the heat of sudden anger, Mamata does not nurse her grudges for long. In support of their argument, they point to the rehabilitation of Congress leaders like Somen Mitra, who used to be diehard Mamata-baiters, and are now part of the Trinamool Congress.

Another disturbing tendency, and one that underlines Mamata's authoritarian streak, was her demand for President's Rule in Bengal. As a partner in the NDA, Mamata repeatedly urged the prime minister to dismiss the Left Front government, particularly after the violent elections in Panskura, in which

Trinamool and CPI-M cadres clashed, leaving scores dead and many seriously injured. After her party's phenomenal victory in the 2009 Lok Sabha elections, and renewed violence in her state afterwards, Mamata asked the UPA government to slap Article 356 on West Bengal. She argued that the state government was violating the Constitution and committing atrocities against Muslims, women, Scheduled Castes and Scheduled Tribes; governance had completely broken down. The Centre, she said, cannot remain a mute spectator. Interestingly, both the NDA and the UPA indulged Mamata as they would a child who was making somewhat unreasonable demands; both governments made the appropriate noises, but never acted on them.

Mamata grapples with a set of contradictory personality traits. Her dictatorial relationship with her party—rudderless without her—coexists with her allowing autonomy to allies outside her own party. The non-Trinamool people who agitated alongside Mamata in Singur and Nandigram do not cast her as an inflexible authoritarian leader. Those peasant movements, so vital to Mamata, would have floundered along the way had the Trinamool president tried to impose her diktat there. 'Mamata always allowed the Singur Krishi Jami Raksha Committee a lot of autonomy. You cannot be a dictator if you can work so successfully with so many different organizations and parties, individuals,' said Pradip Banerjee. So is the skin of a democrat only for the 'outsiders'—the intellectuals, artistes and activists who were drawn to the Trinamool following Singur and Nandigram? I've heard of two incidents that may help us understand this better.

In the days after Lalgarh, there was much discontent in Bengal over the presence of security forces. Amid spiralling controversy over joint security operations in Jangalmahal, Mamata was demanding that the police and paramilitary forces be replaced with the army in the area. She was planning to raise her demand at a public meeting when Pradip Banerjee, among the leading figures of the Singur agitation, told her that they cannot support the entry of the army. He told Mamata that she should stick solely to her demand for withdrawal of security forces. Initially reluctant, Mamata eventually yielded to the wishes of her allies by not bringing up the matter at the rally.

The second incident relates to the controversy arising out of the Trinamool Congress's continuing tiff with Kabir Suman. A three-member delegation of college teachers, including Sujato Bhadra, met Mamata to discuss the matter, which the media was playing up every day. 'We requested her not to go to the media with her complaints against Kabir Suman, not to talk to third parties but directly to Suman. We also told her not to take any organizational action against him,' said Bhadra. Mamata was angry at the request. 'But I must say she never went to the media with her charges against Suman; not even after his book came out, triggering so much controversy.' Bhadra also said that Mamata took Kabir Suman to Pranab Mukherjee, so that he could present his doubts and questions about Operation Green Hunt before the minister.

But Kabir Suman, in *Nishaaner Naam Tapasi Malik*, presents the other side of the picture: 'Following the entry of the joint security forces in Lalgarh and the attacks on tribals, I decided to stand at the gate of Parliament House with a poster demanding the withdrawal of the security forces. Mamata SMSed that she would not allow it. She also said that Maoists too were killing people.'[4] It is worth recalling, in connection with this, Mamata's own defiance of the Congress many decades ago and her going into Lok Sabha with the 'TA-TA to TADA' poster. The shoe was now clearly on the other foot. Despite his repeated requests to the Trinamool Congress president, she did not allow Suman to go ahead with his peaceful protest.

Suman's SMS to Mamata on 18 February 2010 read: 'Please allow me this (protesting at the entry of Parliament House with this poster). I am not causing any disturbance anywhere. You know I was not interested in MPship. I was a free man. But now I am a prisoner. I agreed to contest because you insisted. I have my conscience. I support the UPA, but I oppose this war on our tribals and marginalized people. I can't live with it. Time is running out.'[5] Realizing that Mamata wouldn't budge from her position, Suman finally messaged her asking her to expel him from the party. It is a text that Mamata could well have, in an earlier time, sent to her own party bosses: 'I am a person from the democratic movement. I have no political ambition. Nor have I come from the TMC. You have pressurized me to be here, something I never wanted. I will definitely protest in my own way. You all or anybody else can kill me. I am not scared. On 23rd February, I will stand at the entry of the House with the poster. Expel me. I will abide by the decision.'[6] In response, the Trinamool leadership informed Suman that the party would take a decision after its parliamentary wing had discussed the matter. The meeting, scheduled for February–March 2010, does not seem to have taken place. Turning out to be more 'obedient' than Mamata was in the 1990s, Suman chose not to go ahead with his solo public protest.

To cite another instance of Mamata's high-handedness: On the eve of the 2009 Lok Sabha elections, the Party for

Democratic Socialism (PDS), which had firmly stood by Mamata in the Singur-Nandigram movements, decided to go it alone. 'For more than two years, PDS stood by the land movement led by the Trinamool Congress in West Bengal in order that this movement moves in the right direction and produces no negative results. It was expected that TMC will show magnanimity and respect to the friends of the movement about seat sharing in the coming parliament polls. Unfortunately, this is not happening. PDS has, therefore, decided to contest the coming Parliament elections of its own and support formation of a responsible secular government at the Centre,' a PDS press release announced.

Perversely, there are those who argue that, in a party like the Trinamool, Mamata's ability to maintain absolute control may be the only way to rein in the undesirable elements. Their numbers multiplied as the assembly elections drew near and the ruling CPI-M seemed to be falling behind in the race. There were rumours that even members of the feared Harmad Vahini—violent party cadres roaming the countryside on motorbikes, policing borders of all kinds—were crossing over to the Trinamool. The opportunists in the CPI-M, having wormed their way in, hoping for privilege, were now queuing up before the office of the 'party of the future'. 'We are aware of what is going on. This will be taken care of later,' Trinamool MP Sudip Bandyopadhyay said. 'Currently, Mamata Banerjee is soft-pedalling the issue of the entry of unwanted people. A decision has been taken to set up a five-member committee to weed out the rogue elements after the assembly results are out. The new entrants will be thoroughly screened,' Bhadra said.

The argument, however, is that Mamata needs that autocratic

streak to keep her party running the way she wants it to. Let us step back a little to understand this.

As the elections drew nearer, there were daily reports of the murder of a worker of one party or the other; houses of rivals were burnt; offices were ransacked; university campuses turned into arenas for student sorties. Knives were unsheathed and blood flowed freely and, the following day, the respective parties mourned their dead by carrying the bodies in public processions. Some, like the Trinamool Congress, described this as 'breakdown of law and order', recalling the dangerous streets and alleys of Bihar during Lalu Prasad's tenure. One of the decisive steps that Nitish Kumar took after assuming office was to deal with these lawbreakers who were doing what they would at will. Under his strict vigilance, the law and order situation improved dramatically.

In West Bengal, however, the quality of violence was different—and more difficult to deal with—stitched as it was into the fabric of the state's politics. Mamata wasn't just confronted with a bad law and order situation. She had inherited a political culture whose defining characteristic, before and after 1977, was its running thread of violence. Democratic discourse had given way to competing political players slugging it out with bullets and knives. The Trinamool cadre too is trained in this brutal turf-war culture. Making a change here would be equally, if not more, challenging than edging the CPI-M out of Writers' Buildings. The questions is, will Mamata rise above the easy temptation of an eye-for-an-eye settling of scores? More importantly, will she wield her characteristically heavy hand to restrain party workers who may be indulging their craving for political vendetta?

According to some party leaders, now that the long-established hegemony of the CPI-M is finally broken, the

Trinamool cadre—long forced to play on the back foot—is itching for revenge. Though the Trinamool Congress workers, even in the Opposition, are well equipped in the politics of violence, the CPI-M, particularly its armed militia with the backing of the government and the police, clearly has an upper hand. The killing of nine villagers at Netai by members of the CPI-M's armed militia—who accused the dead of being Maoists—in January 2011 is just one of many such instances. In response to Home Minister P. Chidambaram's repeated requests to Buddhadeb Bhattacharjee to disband his party's armed cadres, the chief minister argued that they need to continue in order to counter the 'Trinamool–Maoist' nexus.

Mamata, however, can ill afford to allow the killings and counter-killings to go on. She does not want to carry on the legacy of the CPI-M's political culture. As she was poised on the threshold of power, Mamata started speaking the language of transition. 'Badla naa badal chai' (not revenge, we want change). 'Mamata Banerjee would not want violence. A word from her would stop it. But the crucial question is whether it would be possible for her to keep a strict watch on every corner, in the remote villages,' a Trinamool leader told me.

The Congress's factional feuds too, in keeping with the party's tradition, could well become virulent with the Left Front's departure. In the second week of March 2011, rival factions of the West Bengal Youth Congress violently clashed with each other over the election of the president. The faction led by Deepa Dasmunshi, MP from Raiganj in North Dinajpur, went on a rampage following the election of Mausam Benazir Noor, MP from the Malda North constituency, and the defeat of Dasmunshi's candidate Arindam Bhattacharya.

So far, the new ruling party has shown amazing restraint in not letting the quest for revenge take an upper hand. Incidents of political violence and vendetta killings have been few and far between.

A related question is how Mamata will define her party's relationship with the Maoists in the changed situation; and equally, how the Maoists will behave in the new political regime. The polls show that the people of West Bengal do not believe the CPI-M's allegation of a Mamata–Maoist collaborative engagement. Mamata has demanded an end to the joint operations by the Central and state forces in the Jangalmahal region and has also urged the Maoists to come to the negotiating table for talks. Even at the Lalgarh meeting on 9 August 2010, Mamata called for laying down arms. But now that she is in power, the decision on withdrawing security force operations is her government's to take. A retraction of her former position would be hard to make.

If the hard-hitting statements by Maoist leader Kishenji are any indication, Mamata is treading on thin ground. Kishenji's biting attack came in the wake of Mamata's vow to 'throw' the Maoists out of West Bengal in January 2010. This is what Kishenji said in a fax message: 'Mamata used the people's movement at Singur and Nandigram to reach the corridors of power at the Centre and now she is dreaming of the chief minister's chair at the cost of people's interest. It sounds like the threats of Buddhadeb Bhattacharjee and P. Chidambaram. Let Mamata try to tarnish Maoists and dispatch forces to suppress a people's movement. The red flag will continue to fly in "Jungle mahal" which she cannot resist and which will bring change in Bengal. It is a matter of surprise that Mamata herself speaks against the people's movement to strengthen the hands of CPI (M) raiders when the people's rights are being established.' Raking up Mamata's political follies of the the past, Kishenji asked, 'Why has she joined hands with a fascist party like the Congress or a communal outfit like the BJP?'

Given the ideology of Maoist politics, Mamata's call to them to abandon armed struggle and join parliamentary democracy is not likely to find acceptance. Kishenji's message indicates that the Maoists are likely to step up pressure on the Trinamool government to withdraw security forces. For this, Mamata will also have to negotiate with the top brass of the UPA government, including the prime minister and the home minister. Moreover, the basic issue of economic revival and development are loaded with the possibility of conflict. Mamata and the Maoists could also clash on the question of industrialization. For Mamata, working in collaboration with industrialists is imperative to getting the economy up on its feet. She has made a beginning in this direction by fielding prominent faces of corporate India, like Amit Mitra—recipient of the Padma Shri award and former general secretary of the Federation of Indian Chambers of Commerce and Industries—in the assembly elections.

8

A Chief Minister in Waiting

Mamata's worries are only going to get worse. She won a decisive mandate on one plinth alone: hope. In the Indian democratic set-up, elections are held every five years, and governments change every five or ten years. The burden of winning does not hang as heavy as it does for the Trinamool, even if the winner were in the Opposition before the elections. West Bengal, though, had forgotten the flavour of change, an essential ingredient to cooking the broth of electoral democracy.

For the people of the state as well as the Trinamool, the situation is as intimidating as it is exhilarating. Veteran actor Victor Banerjee wrote in a recent newspaper article: 'Mamata will be in charge. She is a veritable Kalighat pataka that has trained the guns on the perpetrators of Bengal's misfortunes. What's more, she has the guts and the ability to deliver what we need most: a restoration of our faith and belief in ourselves.'[1] That is a lot to ask of the Trinamool president.

But it has been done before. Nitish Kumar has managed to end Bihar's long stagnation. With careful social engineering and a rhetoric rooted in the politics of inclusion, Kumar has brought about the resurgence of Bihari asmita (pride), a feeling that he himself is emblematic of. According to a Trinamool leader, Mamata's politics too is inclusive. She likes to draw in as many sections of people as possible. She has alliances with different groups, people of different political faiths, intellectuals, artistes and industrialists. These allies of hers come from different, often conflicting, streams of political and social consciousness. Mamata, it is clear, is trying to break from the CPI-M's partisan 'us and them' politics.

The problem is that forging inclusive partnerships was easier when all her allies were united against the overarching objective of ending the three-decade-old Left Front rule. Now that the common objective has been achieved, it is time to meet the aspirations that had propelled diverse groups towards Mamata. She may find that their terms of support are now changing. To balance the contradictions arising from such varied, even conflicting, aspirations will be a tight-rope walk for the Trinamool chief.

There is another story too among Mamata's allies. Those who joined her in the momentum and idealism of the land movements set the benchmark a bit too high, like thirty-six-year-old Barnali Mukherjee. In the thick of the Singur movement, Mukherjee had joined Mamata on her fast, and was severely beaten by the police. For her, Singur and Nandigram were ideological battles and Mamata Banerjee its political or electoral face. Refusing to accept the Trinamool Congress's alliance with the Congress—to her, the 'captain of globalization'—in the 2009 general elections, Barnali distanced herself from the party.

I have mentioned before that the political culture of the state must undergo fundamental change, perhaps even a complete overhaul—no doubt a tall order. But the phenomenon of change cannot be understood unidimensionally. 'Paribartan' has come to mean different things to different stakeholders, many of whom have made a radical electoral shift. To the Paschim Banga Khet Mazdoor Samiti (PBKMS), a trade union that was at the forefront of the Singur and Nandigram movements, and has been working on the ground in Bengal for many years now, change primarily means an expansion in the democratic space for negotiation, discussion and elimination of muscle and money power. To this end, PBKMS members plunged into a bid to overthrow the Left Front, but they are sceptical about the Trinamool Congress's true political ideology.

For the Association for Protection of Democratic Rights (APDR), 'change' means providing human rights the status it has been denied for over thirty years. Mamata's past stance on human rights issues has raised their hopes. In *Struggle for Existence*, Mamata devoted an entire chapter, titled 'Fight for Human Rights', to the issue. Protesting a string of deaths in police custody in 1995, Mamata began what she called a 'holy war' in defence of human rights. Sit-in demonstrations and Janatar Darbars (people's courts) were organized and sustained for twenty-one days. The court began at ten every morning, with people handing in their letters of complaints and allegations. Mamata personally went through the letters: retired teachers starving because their pensions had not been paid; employees of the state government community centre being paid a measly sum of ₹50 a month; a young student being able to retrieve his mark sheet only nine years after he passed an examination. 'Our dharna platform became a sanctuary of people's blessings and love during those twenty-one days. I had not realized how time had flown by. I had not slept even for a single night and not touched a grain of rice for those twenty-one days. Bathing was the biggest problem I faced. The NTC office was right across the road and the employees cooperated with sincerity. I used to use their bathroom before six in the morning for my bath and after the day's work was over I would go over to change into fresh clothes.'[2] The APDR will surely hold her to this commitment in her role as chief minister.

For Mahasweta Devi, 'change' means providing the deprived and the needy their basic entitlements, not acquiring land by force, and allowing people to live with honour and dignity. At the other end of the spectrum are the industrialists who had once lauded Buddhadeb for his aggressive pursuit of industrialization. Now they are looking with hope towards the leader whom they had, not quite so long ago, denounced as 'anti-industry'. Their prediction that Tata's exit from Singur would turn Mamata's electoral and political ambitions to ash has come to naught; they are now hoping that the new establishment will extend a hand of friendship to private investors. The new chief minister has already initiated interactions with industrialists and businesspersons.

'Change must be viewed from the eyes of the weakest and the most oppressed. Change cannot be viewed from the eyes of the privileged. Change is not merely replacing one party with another,' the PBKMS wrote in a statement in 2010. Right now, this is not so different from Mamata's own rhetoric. But how long will she stay loyal to these principles, now that she has reached the destination she longed for all her life? Groups like PBKMS and APDR were deeply involved with the popular struggles over land in Bengal and they are hoping for a transformation of land acquisition policies. The human rights question, especially vis-à-vis political violence, might be difficult to resolve unless Mamata manages to dislodge that political culture which is firmly entrenched in the state.

Friends and Foes

The CPI-M has been gasping for breath for a while now, soothing its frayed nerves, telling itself that things were not as dark as they seemed. It was aware that losing West Bengal would be like being hit by a tsunami, in one stroke destroying the only stable ground the party had in all of India. The prospect of defeat was made more bitter because it would have to concede to an adversary it had attacked, abused and dismissed in the worst possible terms. It was not something the party bosses wanted to consider.

After thirty-four years of power during which the party could have made West Bengal a model state for governance, suddenly Chief Minister Buddhadeb Bhattacharjee suddenly started distributing bicycles among girls. Was he taking a cue from Bihar Chief Minister Nitish Kumar, who is believed to have firmed up his support among women that way? The West Bengal government distributed 33,000 cycles among ninth standard girl students in the North and South 24 Parganas, and 14,000 for tribal girls in three districts of north Bengal. The chief minister said that he hoped the girls would now be able to study properly. One wonders what had tied the CPI-M's hands for three decades and more, but the chief minister was clearly oblivious to irony. The question that begs to be asked, of course, is what good cycles will do in a state whose educational system is in a shambles.

The CPI-M's desperation was obvious. Its leaders, at one point in the election campaign, threatened to rake up a case pending against Mamata dating back to 1994. Then a Youth Congress activist, Mamata was demonstrating outside the district magistrate's office in Barasat. The protest triggered a scuffle between the police and Congress demonstrators and the Barasat police lodged a complaint, based on which a charge sheet was filed in April 1999. The court issued a warrant for Mamata's arrest in 2005. By then, she had formed the Trinamool Congress, participated in assembly and parliamentary polls three times each, and had been appointed railway minister twice. The CPI-M, then confident of its supreme power, had not bothered with the pending case. In 2011, however, the party's North 24 Parganas District Secretariat member Amitava Nandy suddenly dredged up the case, filing a complaint before the Election Commission. In his petition, Nandy questioned Mamata's right to 'roam around freely', even after being charge-sheeted. He asked the Election Commission to issue a non-bailable warrant against Mamata.

This was, of course, yet another indication of the CPI-M's inability to come to terms with the logic of electoral democracy. Once the victims of political cases themselves, the CPI-M of today is a far cry from the party it had been in those heady years leading up to 1977. Chief Minister Buddhadeb Bhattacharjee stepped in to make a sensible interjection, perhaps realizing that going after Mamata would only further damage the party at that stage. 'There is no question of arresting or harassing Mamata Banerjee before the assembly elections,' Buddhadeb told a press conference.

As I've said before, the Bengal of today recalls in some ways the Bihar that survived fifteen years of Rashtriya Janata Dal rule. But the rot in Bengal is deeper, both because of the length of the CPI-M's tenure and its unique organizational structure. So the immense enthusiasm that greeted Mamata should also be viewed in the context of over three decades of denial. The multiplicity of objectives of people's desires can perhaps be understood when framed within the magnitude of this colossal denial. 'My support for Mamata is driven by the objective situation in West Bengal. After so many years of Left Front rule, even today people do not have ration cards, large parts of rural areas are without electricity, roads, safe drinking water. The situation in the tribal areas is even worse,' Mahasweta Devi told me. The prelude to change is clouded, though, as the author, looking out of her window, sees that the garbage dump outside her house has not been removed by the Kolkata Municipal Corporation, now controlled by the Trinamool Congress. 'The CPI-M created the dump, and the Trinamool is maintaining it!' she says. Like many others, she does not have unquestioning faith in Mamata's party, but does believe in her.

The dominant impression seems to be that Mamata will remote-control her cabinet and its ministers. 'Mamata is not a good administrator,' a former Congress and now Trinamool Congress leader said to me, adding: 'All along, she has played negative politics. Undoubtedly, her honesty is her biggest virtue. She will never take money from a businessman. But as far as administrative acumen is concerned…'

On the political front, Mamata's uneasy, fractured alliance with the Congress portends conflict and acrimony for the future. The Trinamool is acutely conscious of this undercurrent of hostility with its ally. 'Much of what we can achieve will depend on our victory margin. We need a high margin to be able to work without hitches,' a Trinamool leader told me before the elections. The seat-sharing formula with the Congress, finally cemented on the eve of the elections, was beset with hitches from the beginning, with the Congress demanding over ninety seats, grossly out of proportion with its strength, and Mamata agreeing to part with around sixty. Finally, the Congress had to settle for sixty-five seats.

The Congress, for its part, was uncomfortable with the prospect that the Trinamool may get a whopping majority that would make it, for all practical purposes, independent of the alliance. Which is, of course, precisely what Mamata hoped for. Her relations with the West Bengal Pradesh Congress Committee (WBPCC) president Manas Bhunia are prickly underneath their laboured camaraderie in public. During the run-up to the elections, Manas even complained to journalists that Mamata was not answering his calls. Less than a month ahead of the elections, the WBPCC president was camping in Delhi petitioning the entire Congress leadership, from Rahul Gandhi and Ahmed Patel to Janardhan Poojary and Pranab Mukherjee, to drive a hard bargain with Mamata.

Rahul Gandhi's visit to West Bengal in 2010 provoked Mamata into taking a few characteristic digs at the 'prince' of Indian politics. The Trinamool chief is usually circumspect about what she says about members of the Gandhi family, if only because of her high regard for Rajiv Gandhi. 'We are not a rarely seen seasonal flower [*Amra dumurer phool noi*] that we will appear like cuckoos before elections, chirp and fly away. [...] The road I travel is at my fingertips. I know its characteristics. Throughout the year, I am with the people. I know their problems and they know me. I understand their language,' she said.[3] Stressing that Rahul has her blessing, Mamata said that he is yet to cut his teeth in politics. Predictably Mamata's comments led Manas to rush to Rahul's defence.

The tussle over seat-sharing with the Congress was finally sorted out, with Sonia Gandhi overruling the West Bengal unit's peevishness. The rest of the party, as expected, fell in line. Through the seat-sharing squabbles, Mamata showed a new maturity, neither queering the pitch, nor giving in to the Congress's unreasonable bullying. Perhaps a decade earlier, she would have allowed her stormy temper an upper hand. This time, she waited patiently for the Congress high command to untangle the knots, while retaining full command of the situation.

The Way Ahead

Post-elections, one of the big challenges before Mamata was to pick the right people for her cabinet. 'This is one area where there is a deficit of talent in the Trinamool Congress,' said a close associate. Knowing this, Mamata decided to institute a body along the lines of Sonia Gandhi's National Advisory Council, comprising experts and specialists in their respective fields. In addition, the Trinamool chief discussed the revival of the Vidhan Parishad, the Upper House of the West Bengal assembly. This will give Mamata an opportunity to bring in skilled people in advisory capacities. For instance, economist Abhirup Sarkar, who turned down Mamata's offer of candidacy, may find a place in the Upper House. The list of Trinamool Congress candidates who contested the elections indicates Mamata's search for educated, skilled people, who are experienced in governance and administration.

Mamata's politics, her colleagues say, is inclusive in character, and the party's list of candidates—former bureaucrats, police officials, artistes, teachers, corporate executives—is reflective of this. Amit Mitra was pitted against the Left Front's finance minister Asim Dasgupta in the Kharda constituency; former chief secretary Manish Gupta against none other than then chief minister Buddhadeb Bhattacharjee; theatre director Bratya Basu against former minister Gautam Deb, projected by the CPI-M as its new reformed face.

The candidates' list had a fair share of names from outside the Trinamool. Manish Gupta had served the Left Front government throughout his career. In fact, it was Jyoti Basu who appointed him chief secretary in 1998, a post he held until he retired in 2001. He is allegedly implicated in two horrifying attacks on Mamata in 1993. The first was when she stormed Writers' Buildings and held a dharna outside Jyoti Basu's chamber, demanding justice for a rape victim; and the second was when the police indiscriminately fired upon Youth Congress activists, killing thirteen of them, an incident I discussed earlier. If Manish Gupta is expected to recast West Bengal's administration, Amit Mitra is meant to attract investors and investment to West Bengal. The Trinamool also fielded former IPS officers Aboni Joardar, H.A. Safwi, Rachpal Singh and Sultan Singh, former IAS officer Dipak Ghosh and retired judge Noor Alam Chowdhury.

School and college teachers had for a long time been the CPI-M's backbone of support. The Trinamool made sure to field a number of teachers during the elections—among others, Jiban Mukherjee, a former professor of history at Vidyasagar College; Braja Mohan Majumdar, headmaster of Howrah's Vivekananda Institution for the last twenty-eight years and recipient of the President's award for his work as teacher; and Padma Mahato, teacher in Sandeshkhali Primary School.

All of this appears to be in keeping with Mamata Banerjee's stated objective of promoting a culture that transcends party affiliations and interests. In fact, on the eve of the elections, the Trinamool chief went to the extent of saying that she did not mind if student organizations functioned outside the control of political parties. On innumerable occasions, she has maintained that everything need not be 'politicized'.

Given these lofty aims, Mamata could find herself in a Nitish Kumar-like quandary. It took the Bihar chief minister a full five-year term to reap the benefits of his policies of change. He marked out his areas of priority. According to experts, the improvement in the law and order situation provided women and the minorities with a sense of security, and this was reflected in their all-out support for Nitish Kumar. The conviction of the rich and powerful, including some from Nitish Kumar's own party, the conviction of the Bhagalpur riot criminals and compensation for riot victims were all perceived as markers of his sincerity. It must also be said that the Nitish bubble is, in part, created by a media-driven euphoria that, like in the case of Gujarat's Narendra Modi, has enthusiastically promoted a 'development' story. Reports of disaffection among the people do not make it to the news.

Mamata, in her endeavour to transform West Bengal, will have to be conscious of these contradictory political and developmental challenges: while she is currently on the right side of the media and different sections of the people, she may easily have to betray one constituency to hold on to the other.

Changing the political culture of the state is one of Mamata's highest priorities. The Trinamool president has hinted that she could reopen the files of the many commission reports not made public till date. Between 1977 and 1979, the West Bengal state government had instituted twenty-one commissions to probe allegations of police atrocities. Barring a few, findings of most of the reports were kept under wraps. Mamata has stressed that she will not play the politics of vendetta, but at the same time, she has categorically announced her intention to reopen inquiries into explosive cases like Sain Bari, the murder of Forward Bloc leader Hemanta Basu in the 1970s and the killings in Chhoto Angaria and Netai between 2001 and 2011. I'd like to stop and look back at these bloody histories of Bengal.

On 17 March 1970, the two Sain brothers, Pranab and Moloy, and Jiten Roy, their private tutor, were gruesomely murdered, sending shivers through the state. The attackers set the Sain home on fire and then speared the two brothers, smearing the mother's face with their blood. The family was targeted for its allegiance to the Congress. Three CPI-M leaders were accused of conspiring, organizing and committing the carnage, and charged under sections 148, 149, 307, 302, 438 and 300 of the Indian Penal Code. Swarnalata Josh, sister of the deceased, who was visiting her parents' house on the day of the murder, and survived the attack, wants the case reopened. On 17 March 2010, Opposition members belonging to the Trinamool and the Congress staged a walkout in the state assembly after Speaker H.A. Halim turned down their demand for an adjournment motion on the Sain Bari murder case. The Speaker later argued that an adjournment motion could be allowed only on recent matters and not an incident that had occurred forty years ago. 'Several Opposition members rushed to the well of the House, shouting slogans and demanding the resignation of the Industry Minister, Mr Nirupam Sen, an accused in the case. They also demanded the arrest of Mr Sen, along with former CPI-M MP Mr Anil Basu and party central committee member Mr Benoy Konar, who had also been named accused. Mr Sen was in the House when the ruckus went on,' a newspaper reported.[4] The Sain Bari case has become an icon of the chilling politics of vendetta and violence that has now become synonymous with West Bengal. It is quite certain that the Trinamool will reopen the case.

Mamata has also often criticized the fact that the Left Front government did not probe the murder of Forward Bloc leader Hemanta Basu (who was stabbed to death as he stepped outside his house on the eve of the 1971 elections) in spite of the many decades it was in power and could have initiated action. Then there is the case where, in 2001, CPI-M supporters burnt to death eleven Trinamool workers in Chhoto Angaria village in East Medinipur. In 2007, the additional district and sessions judge of West Medinipur framed charges against CPI-M leaders Tapan Ghosh and Sukur Ali in connection with the murders. The latest in the unending series of CPI-M-sponsored murders happened in Netai village near Lalgarh. CBI investigations have revealed that the CPI-M set up a camp of armed mercenaries who opened fire on innocent villagers, killing seven of them on 7 January 2011.

For the CPI-M, Mamata's declaration that she will bring the guilty to book must be nerve-wracking. The party had not factored in the possibility of losing an election; otherwise, these cases could have been raked up, reopened and closed many times in the past three decades. But, for the most part, it appears that Mamata Banerjee will focus on reviving governance and depoliticizing the administration. Her associates say the Trinamool chief is studying different models of governance in India, including Gujarat and Karnataka. Her allies, Left-wing individuals, cultural personalities and human rights activists are bringing her books on the 'second green revolution', genetics in agriculture, industrialization, Barack Obama, Binayak Sen, civil liberties and the like. We are yet to see whether these wide-ranging influences inform her decisions in government.

Epilogue

D-Day: 13 May 2011

Leading up to that stirring moment of transfer of power, the atmosphere was taut with anticipation, electric with hope. Mamata Banerjee, the face of the tectonic political shift, had campaigned on Kolkata's streets, covering mile after mile on foot. Women and men in countless numbers trailed her—falling over each other to catch a closer glimpse of the woman, exceptional in her ordinariness, the woman who was about to make history.

All indications were that the Marxists had lost the searing eyeball-to-eyeball challenge even before the final die was cast. But not even for a second did the possibility of an ignominious defeat tame the hubris of the CPI-M leaders. Not for a moment did it make them pause in their tracks or instil in them a sense of genuine humility, a willingness to introspect without whittling down the exercise to a mechanical computation of the ills besetting the party. On the contrary, all through the campaign, the CPI-M showed to the people the face they were only too familiar with: brazen, unyielding. Loath to let go, belligerent leaders launched into an unfettered and wilful campaign that plunged new depths in its personal attacks and political rhetoric. Nothing was out of bounds, nothing too indecent or vulgar in the defeated giant's refusal to let go of the frayed reins of control.

Projected as the party's 'face for transformation', Gautam Deb led the attack from the front, leaving Buddhadeb Bhattacharjee to strike a more restrained tone. The top brass tacitly endorsed former CPI-M MP Anil Basu's abusive rant against Mamata, even as they held out perfunctory apologies for him calling her a 'sex worker' and accusing her of entertaining 'American clients'. In Anil Basu's ill-chosen words, the communist government's patriarchy and its blame-everything-on-the-CIA paranoia were once again on view. The public was still reeling from Anil Basu's verbal assaults when Bhattacharjee addressed a public meeting, at which the offending leader, his head held high, was spotted sitting in the front row.

Furious with the media for predicting the CPI-M's electoral defeat, its leaders began to fling around outlandish charges. Biman Bose held forth on 'media terror' at a press conference a day before the results were announced; Gautam Deb accused media houses of taking money and rooting for Mamata. Once in a while, he also brought in the US in his theory of a grand conspiracy to oust Marxism from Bengal. On the ground, support for Mamata was steadily surging. Seemingly oblivious to this celebratory upsurge, the Marxists behaved as if they were in possession of some secret knowledge of a last-minute poll wonder that would end their traumatic ordeal on a less dismal, if not entirely cheerful, note.

By the early afternoon of 13 May 2011, the Left Front regime was faced with its worst electoral performance since 1977. It is one thing to lose power after thirty-four long years, and another entirely to have to depart on a note of such withering defeat. From 235 seats in 2006, the Left Front tumbled to a paltry sixty-two. All of the CPI-M's heavyweight ministers, including the chief minister and the finance minister, lost to political novices. The victorious Trinamool Congress and Congress combine wrested control of Writers' Buildings with a very comfortable 226 seats.

A week later, on the afternoon of 20 May, Mamata was sworn in as West Bengal's chief minister, heading a forty-four-member Trinamool Congress–Congress coalition cabinet.

The Left Front government left in its wake a tangled wreck of a state, with the economy in a shambles, governance in tatters and a highly politicized administration sunk in deep inertia. It was difficult not to travel back in time to June 1977, when Jyoti Basu had taken charge of West Bengal, decimating the Congress and inheriting a state scarred beyond recognition. Then, as now, West Bengal was in a state of acute distress, a state in dire need of revival. Much like the amateur Marxist rulers of the 1970s—who were groomed and skilled in radical politics and not the intricate 'art of governance'—Mamata too is seen as wanting in administrative capability.

Mamata frequently encounters the charge that her party lacks a coherent policy and programme, something that West Bengal critically needs. She has achieved her electoral and political goal, but her transformation from a raw street fighter to the performing head of a troubled state is still to be certified as a success. For that, she will have to deliver on all fronts and transform the political culture in the state.

Right now, Mamata is acutely conscious that the most crucial lap of her journey is pitted with craters every inch of the way.

Within forty-eight hours of the poll results, CPI-M leaders in Delhi and Kolkata began belting out predictable allegations that the Trinamool Congress was killing their workers and setting party offices ablaze. The party sent out press releases replete with warnings of imminent violence sponsored by the new regime. Were these graceless losers, in the dark recesses of their mind, actually hoping for a backlash? In the lead-up to the polls, the party had time and again raised the spectre of a return to the chaotic pre-1977 West Bengal if the regime changed.

But in the immediate aftermath of the polls, the new rulers, for the moment at least, sheathed their anger, their desire to square up with their long-standing opponents. Spectacles of badla would have marred the momentous prelude to Mamata's paribartan. Instead, Mamata repeatedly called for peace and for celebrations that would not hurt others.

In their eagerness to charge the Trinamool Congress with presiding over possible large-scale post-electoral violence, the CPI-M seemed to completely overlook two significant facts about the culture of political violence in the state. Firstly, the communists themselves are responsible for spurring on the violence. To accuse Mamata Banerjee of 'creating' it was, therefore, completely dishonest. Secondly, this culture of violence has left scores of ordinary people—specially in the rural hinterlands—fed up and angry with the Left Front administration. For years, they had been at the receiving end of state violence in different forms, of which Singur, Nandigram, Lalgarh and Netai are but the most prominent examples. Mamata Banerjee need not sanction violence in these parts. If they retaliate with violence against the CPI-M cadre, it will be an explosion of rage. So far though, the Left's predictions that the state will slide deeper into chaos have not been borne out. Incidents of violence in rural Bengal have been sporadic, not organized or politically sanctioned.

THE FUTURE OF THE 'LEFT'

Undoubtedly, much of the narrative for the next five years will depend upon the CPI-M: how the party chooses to behave in the Opposition, how it deals with the trauma of its defeat, and how it redefines its ideological and political framework. So far, there has been no genuine soul-searching by the leadership, who have chosen instead to remain sullen.

Predictably, the party has started talking about its plans to cleanse the organization of all the rot accumulated over the few decades. But the CPI-M's rectification drives are a stale promise. They might provide rhetorical ammunition to party cadre, but have scarcely managed to re-energize the party organizationally. For years, the CPI-M has been holding forth on this commitment to 'purify' itself and, in the same breath, defending the atrocious actions of its cadres and leaders.

Internal churning within the party and its ability to reinvent itself will be crucial to West Bengal's long-term political journey. From the new government's point of view, the tactics and strategies that the CPI-M adopts as the main Opposition will be important. And the CPI-M could play a constructive role and recover some of its lost popularity. Or it could resort to a politics of vendetta and not allow the new government to function. The Opposition will, of course, keep a hawk's eye on any issue of industrialization, especially where it involves conflict over the acquisition of land. This has already come to pass in Sankrail, when protesters from the SFI, the CPI-M's students wing, successfully derailed a rail coach factory project.

Policy and Administration

The decisive shift in political power signals the beginnings of a transformation, one that is yet to gain structure and content. A confident chief minister, from the first day she took charge, has made it clear that providing an efficient, clean, non-partisan administration and good governance is her top priority, alongside bringing in investment, generating employment and working out a viable land policy.

Health and education, two terribly ailing sectors, are top priorities now. Mamata has started making lightning visits to one government hospital after another, each appearing to be in a state worse than the one before. She makes a rapid tour of the hospitals, takes note of the complaints of waiting patients and their relatives, as well as that of the doctors. One of the major blots on the Left Front's record was its indifference to work ethic. Mamata has started toning up the sickly administration through strict, if unpleasant measures.

West Bengal's education system, its colleges and universities—long held hostage to the CPI-M's partisan governance—had mediocre, ill-deserving party appointees lording over them, scripting the epitaphs of these institutions in that process. Presidency College bears testimony to this process of attrition. Barring the state and the party, every other institution in West Bengal, in the classically Marxist sense, has 'withered away'.

As she starts to clean up the frightening mess, Mamata has begun depoliticizing the education system, which in itself is a mammoth task. Aiding the process, undoubtedly, is the fact that her party lacks the Left's intellectual baggage and, therefore, presumably the ability to cram institutions with party cadres.

The Land Question

Even before her landslide victory, Mamata had begun to initiate and consolidate channels of communication with industrialists. Following Durga Puja celebrations in 2010, she played host to top corporates in Kolkata's posh Ballygunge area. Over a hundred invitations were sent out to industrialists and chambers. Among the attendees at Mamata's Bijoya Sammelani were industrialists who share a good rapport with Buddhadeb Bhattacharjee: RPG Enterprise Vice Chairman Sanjeev Goenka, Ambuja Realty Chairman Harsh Neotia, Keventer Group Chairman M.K. Jalan, Tata Ryerson MD and Bengal Chamber of Commerce and Industry President Sandipan Chakraborty, Descon MD S. Radhakrishnan, Acclaris MD Kalyan Kar, and Patton MD Sanjay Budhia.

Mamata has consciously crafted a new image without unsettling her core constituency of supporters. 'She is definitely changing her attitude towards industrialists. I remember in the 1990s some industrialists wanted to talk to Mamata, then railway minister, on policies. But she had shown no interest,' said Krishna Bose, adding, 'I noticed the change in her when she came to meet me on my birthday this time. It was a social gathering. Mamata went around meeting everybody, exchanging pleasantries.'

A year after the Tatas exited from Singur, G.S. Meakan, a senior representative of the company, attended a function where

Mamata ceremonially laid the foundation for an automobile hub near Shalimar Railway Station close to Kolkata. Senior executives from other automobile companies too were present. 'I welcome you to the logistic hub, to the auto hub and also for setting up joint ventures with the railways, if you are interested,' Mamata said, informing them that a committee had been set up for the public–private partnership ventures of her ministry. 'We have land,' she said pithily.[1]

Mamata has made clear that she will not backtrack on the promises she made from the battlefields of Singur and Nandigram. The UPA government is looking for her support to pass the amended Land Acquisition Bill (2011) because Mamata's objections to the earlier draft had delayed its passage. Though yet to fine-tune her position, Mamata now seems ready to back the draft, which has been further amended.

The Trinamool Congress wants no government intervention in the acquisition of land, unless it is for national interest, like defence and infrastructure development. Mamata wants negotiated settlement on land price and adequate compensation based on prevailing market rates, giving back part of the land to the original owners after it has been developed for commercial use.

With the land struggles breaking out everywhere across the country, there is speculation that once Mamata agrees to the current bill she will save the Congress-led UPA government from some of the heat it is facing for the delay in passing the legislation. It is difficult to say for sure yet whether she will go back on her word. But it seems unlikely that Mamata will act in a manner that jeopardizes the very constituency that turned the tide her way in 2006.

Mamata has lost no time in setting up a two-member Land Commission for West Bengal, one of the members being the former bureaucrat Debabrata Bandyopadhyay, also one of the main authors of Operation Barga, the land reform programme that gave the Left Front its impressive longevity. He is now advising Mamata on how to deal with the explosive land situation. Her speech in Parliament against the Land Acquisition Bill showed her knowledge of, and familiarity with, these controversial issues. Bandyopadhyay is known for his support for ownership rights for sharecroppers, a policy left unrealized during the long rule of the Left Front government. It is likely that he will, in his advisory capacity, pitch for the implementation of this long-delayed reform.

Soon after coming to power in June 2011, the West Bengal assembly passed the Singur Land Rehabilitation and Development Bill to reclaim the land given by the Left Front government to the Tatas for the Nano factory, and to return 400 acres to the peasant-owners. This was one of Mamata's primary electoral promises. The Tatas moved court to stall the bill, contesting that they had been forced to abandon the land, facing resistance from the peasants and the Trinamool Congress. Responding to the Tatas' plea, the Supreme Court, in an interim order, asked the West Bengal government not to return the land to the peasants.

The land imbroglio will undoubtedly be one of the most difficult challenges before the new chief ninister and her government. She has already made it clear that on no account will her government seize land from peasants without their consent. While on the one hand, her cabinet (with its ministers from diverse backgrounds, many of them not from the Trinamool) may finally depoliticize the administration, on the other hand, having a committed private sector cheerleader like Amit Mitra in the finance ninister's seat, or a bureaucrat with a controversial past like Manish Gupta as minister for development and planning, may throw up interests colliding with the political goals of the Trinamool Congress.

Working through Paradoxes

Such contradictions seem to bolster critics—from the Left and elsewhere—who claim that the Trinamool Congress neither has any policy perspectives, nor any ideological commitments. But then, Mamata Banerjee has never been one to fight politics purely through policy. It has been my endeavour in this book to demonstrate that she is, indeed, not an ideologically motivated person. But I have also illustrated the rapid transformation both she and her party have undergone in the past few years, especially since 2006. From the influx of culturally and politically sensitive intellectuals, to the entry of former Marxist-Leninists and the opening up of dialogues with human rights activists and non-Left-Front trade unions, Mamata has come a fair distance. She does have a political constituency. Moreover, these varied groups and individuals—from Abhirup Sarkar and Sujato Bhadra to Bratya Basu—have fresh ideas from which she may benefit.

As I write this, towards the end of 2011, the euphoria of transfer of power is still lingering. Mamata Banerjee is handing out a talking point nearly every day. She is bolstering people's soaring expectations with her lightning visits to hospitals; she continues to live in her Kalighat residence; she drives around in her old black Santro rather than the official bulletproof Scorpio. Mamata's personal character and conduct are continuously being woven into the larger narrative of transformation in West Bengal.

However, in keeping with the general order of democratic transaction, this euphoria will wane to make room for hard-headed, prosaic calculations. And precisely because she was able to drum up euphoria like this, riding on the aspirations of a restless people, Mamata runs the risk of encountering swift reprisal if she takes away the hope she has held out.

Bringing in 'paribartan'—defined not merely as a transfer of state power but as providing a genuinely alternative political, social, intellectual, cultural platform—may indeed be as much, if not more, of a challenge than unseating the Left Front government.

Here, the question of the 'future of the Left' in India arises once again. The mainstream media, with its tendency to simplify, posed a series of questions as the election results came in on 13 May: is communism dead, is Marxism over, does the Left have any future, shouldn't we now simply give in to the order of things? The CPI-M must have been pleased with the formulation of these questions for they seemed to concede that it was indeed the only representative of the 'Left' in India. However, the reality is that the CPI-M is only the parliamentary face of the Left. Outside the formal party structures, countless organizations on the ground are fighting the greed and wily methods of the corporates that seek to further dispossess the poor of their land. These groups and individuals are fighting on many fronts, risking their lives to assert their right to information, fighting the violence of military occupation, caste and communal backlash. Maybe they will now, finally, emerge as the 'real' Left.

Paradoxically, Mamata Banerjee, who originally comes from

a relatively 'rightist' political lineage, has already appropriated much of the political and cultural space that had once belonged exclusively to the Left. The demarcations between the Right and the Left have become increasingly fuzzy in West Bengal. The 2011 elections have set in motion a set of dynamics that may yet lead to the crystallization of new Left forces. As Mamata Banerjee has time and again said, her fight is not against the Left, but the CPI-M. In fact, she has even expressed her support for certain principles of 'Leftism'.

This perplexing ambivalence, this bucking of stereotypes and of analytical frameworks defines Mamata Banerjee. Her equivocation and the conflicting aspects of her personality set Mamata up as a paradoxical figure, decidedly someone to watch out for in the years to come.

Notes and References

Chapter 1

1. The AICC is the highest decision-making body of the Indian National Congress, henceforth referred to as the Congress or Congress party.
2. Mamata Banerjee, *Struggle for Existence* (Magvisual Priyonkar Publications, 1998: Kolkata), p. 13.
3. Ibid., p. 13.
4. Ibid., p. 13.
5. Ibid., pp. 13–14.
6. As its name indicates, TADA was introduced in 1985 to curb insurgency in Punjab and was in effect till 1995. The Act was widely misused, as is the tendency with many such laws meant to curb terrorism.
7. *Struggle for Existence*, p. 114.
8. Ibid.
9. Ibid., p. 15.
10. Ibid., p. 16.
11. Ibid., p. 4.
12. Mamata Banerjee, *Ekante* (Dey's Publishing, 2003: Kolkata), p. 16.
13. In 2007, Rizwanur Rehman, a thirty-year-old computer graphics engineer, was found dead in mysterious circumstances following his marriage to Priyanka Todi, daughter of industrialist Ashok Todi. Though the police claimed Rizwanur committed suicide, the

Kolkata High Court eventually declared his death to be a murder. The perceived collusion between the police, the state government and the industrialist led to widespread public anger and sharpened the sense of alienation amongst the minority community in the state.
14. Moinak Biswas, 'Changing Scenes', *Sarai Reader 8* (2010: Delhi), p. 196.
15. Ibid., p. 205.
16. Ibid., pp. 196–295.
17. *Ekante*, p. 22.
18. Ibid., p. 22.
19. Ibid., pp. 24–25.
20. Ibid., p. 24.
21. Sumit Sarkar, '"Kaliyug", "Chakri" and "Bhakti": Ramakrishna and His Times', *Economic and Political Weekly* (18 July 1992), p. 1543.
22. Ibid., p. 1544.
23. Ibid., p. 1562.
24. *Ekante*, p. 25.

Chapter 2

1. The state government secretariat in Kolkata.
2. An armed insurrection of peasants, which fundamentally changed the course of Left politics in India.
3. Mamata Banerjee, *Struggle for Existence* (Magvisual Priyonkar Publications, 1998: Kolkata), p. 5.
4. Ibid., p, 4.
5. Ibid., pp. 12–13.
6. Somnath Chatterjee, *Keeping the Faith: Memoirs of a Parliamentarian* (HarperCollins India, 2010: New Delhi), p. 89.
7. *Struggle for Existence*, p. 28.
8. Dwaipayan Bhattacharyya, 'Making and Unmaking of Trinamul Congress', *Economic and Political Weekly* (3–10 April 2004), p. 1530.
9. *Struggle for Existence*, p. 165.
10. Mamata Banerjee, *Trinamool* (Dey's Publishing, 1999: Kolkata), p. 14.
11. *Struggle for Existence*, p. 172.

12. Peoples' Union for Democratic Rights, *Lawless Roads: A Report on TADA 1985-1993* (September 1993).
13. *Struggle for Existence*, p. 38.
14. Krishna Bose, *Parliamenter Andare* (Ananda Publications, Kolkata).
15. *Trinamool*, p. 27.
16. Ibid., p. 28.
17. In 2002, thousands of Muslims were killed in Gujarat during communal violence, as the administration of the BJP chief minister Narendra Modi remained a passive spectator and, according to some, actively aided the massacre of minorities.
18. *Trinamool*, p. 45.
19. In March 2001, an exposé by *Tehelka* (in its earlier avatar as a website), called Operation West End, revealed serious corruption in the NDA government, particularly its defence ministry, leading to the eventual resignation of then defence minister George Fernandes. See *www.tehelka.com/home/20041009/operationwe/investigation1.htm* for details.
20. Mamata Banerjee, *Anubhuti* (Dey's Publishing, 2002: Kolkata), p. 74.
21. Ibid., p. 92.

CHAPTER 3

1. Mamata Banerjee, *Struggle for Existence* (Magvisual Priyonkar Publications, 1998: Kolkata), p. 25.
2. Ibid., p. 26.
3. Uday Basu, 'Shahid Divas Then and Now', *The Statesman* (21 July 2010).
4. Raka Ray, 'Women's Movements and Political Fields: A Comparison of Two Indian Cities', *Social Problems* (Vol. 45, No. 1, 1998), p. 27.
5. Kabir Suman, *Nishaaner Naam Tapasi Malik* (Mitra & Ghosh Publishers Pvt. Ltd, 2010: Kolkata), p. 42.
6. 'Women's Movements and Political Fields', p. 26.
7. Frigga Haug, 'The End of Socialism in Europe: A New Challenge for Socialist Feminism?', *Feminist Review* (No. 39, Autumn 1991), p. 40.

8. www.deccanchronicle.com/channels/cities/kochi/shock-cpm-sindhu-joins-cong-530
9. Mamata Banerjee, *Ekante* (Dey's Publishing, 2003: Kolkata), p. 43.
10. Mamata Banerjee, *Manabik* (Dey's Publishing, 1997: Kolkata), p. 25.
11. *Ekante*, p. 67.
12. 'Believe It! Ministers have Aam Aadmi Assets', *The Economic Times* (10 September 2010).
13. 'Mayawati's Assets Rise from ₹52 crore to 87 crore in 3 Years', *The Times of India*, (27 May 2010).
14. Aditya Nigam, 'The Heterotopias of Dalit Politics: Becoming-Subject and the Consumption Utopia', in *Utopia/Dystopia: Conditions of Historical Possibility* (Princeton University Press, 2010: Princeton), p. 252.
15. Ibid., p. 254–55.
16. *Struggle for Existence*, p. 115.
17. *Ekante*, p. 57.

Chapter 4

1. Mamata Banerjee, *Andoloner Katha* (Dey's Publishing, 2009: Kolkata), p. 54.
2. B. Prasant, 'Who Killed Tapasi Malik at Singur?', *People's Democracy* (6 May 2007).
3. *Andoloner Katha*, p. 102.
4. Ibid., p. 103.
5. Ibid., p. 18.
6. Kabir Suman, *Nishaaner Naam Tapasi Malik* (Mitra & Ghosh Publishers Pvt. Ltd, 2010: Kolkata), p. 80.
7. Kunal Chattopadhyay, 'Violence in Singur', *Mainstream* (Vol. XLV, No. 01, December 2006).
8. *Nishaaner Naam Tapasi Malik*, pp. 42–43.
9. Ibid., pp. 43–44.
10. Ibid., p. 47.
11. *Andoloner Katha*, p. 18.
12. *Nishaaner Naam Tapasi Malik*, p. 94.
13. *Andoloner Katha*, pp. 139–40.

14. Ibid., p. 140.
15. *Nishaaner Naam Tapasi Malik*, p. 135.
16. Ibid., p. 135.

Chapter 5

1. 'Bring Taslima Nasreen Back to Kolkata: Mahasweta Devi', *The Hindu* (23 November 2010).
2. Kabir Suman, *Nishaaner Naam Tapasi Malik* (Mitra & Ghosh Publishers Pvt. Ltd, 2010: Kolkata), p. 21.
3. Ibid.
4. Ibid.
5. 'At Farewell, Gopalkrishna Gandhi Calls for Change in Mindsets', *The Hindu* (14 December 2009).
6. http://specials.rediff.com/election/2006/may/05pinter.htm
7. Nikhat Kazmi, 'Film Fest Opens in Goa, Mamata Steals the Show', *The Times of India* (23 November 2010).
8. Ibid.
9. Ashok Mitra, 'Culture and the Left', *Seminar* (No. 559, March 2006).
10. Ritwik Ghatak, *On the Cultural Front: A Thesis Submitted by Ritwik Ghatak* (Ritwik Memorial Trust, 1996: Kolkata), p. 41.
11. Ibid.
12. Ibid., p. 43.
13. Mamata Banerjee, *Struggle for Existence* (Magvisual Priyonkar Publications, 1998: Kolkata), p. 34.
14. http://jyotibasumemoirs.wordpress.com/2009/04/02/chapter-viii-tebhaga-movement/.
15. Moinak Biswas, 'Changing Scenes', *Sarai Reader 8* (2010: Delhi), p. 201.
16. Asim Chatterjee, 'If You Follow Party Fiats, How are You an Intellectual?', *Anandabazar Patrika* (15 February 2011).

Chapter 6

1. Sreecheta Das, 'Didi Signs in Sabeer Bhatia to Net Voters', *Indian Express* (14 March 2011).

2. Somdatta Basu, 'IIM-C Duo Bags Dream Stint with Trinamool', *Times of India* (10 March 2011).
3. Boris Groys, 'Self-Design and Aesthetic Responsibility', *E-Flux Journal* (June 2009).

Chapter 7

1. Mamata Banerjee, *Struggle for Existence* (Magvisual Priyonkar Publications, 1998: Kolkata), pp. 173–74.
2. Mamata Banerjee, *Jago Bangla* (Dey's Publishing, 2006: Kolkata), p. 146.
3. *Struggle for Existence*, pp. 17–18.
4. Kabir Suman, *Nishaaner Naam Tapasi Malik* (Mitra & Ghosh Publishers Pvt. Ltd, 2010: Kolkata), p. 234.
5. Ibid.
6. Ibid., pp. 235–36.

Chapter 8

1. 'Taking the Wrong Left,' *Indian Express* (9 March 2011).
2. Mamata Banerjee, *Struggle for Existence* (Magvisual Priyonkar Publications, 1998: Kolkata), pp. 145–46.
3. 'Mamata Says She is Not a Seasonal Flower', *The Hindu* (21 September 2010).
4. 'Walkout Over Sain Bari', *The Statesman* (17 March 2011).

Epilogue

1. 'Mamata Invites Investment in Automobile Hub in Kolkata', *The Hindu* (28 November 2009).

Index

Academy of Fine Arts, Kolkata, 123
Achuthanandan, V.S., 72
Advani, L.K., 48, 103
Alipur bomb case (1908), 19
All India Congress Committee (AICC), 1, 30, 42, 44
All India Minority Forum, 115–16
Ambedkar, B.R., 83–84
Andolan, 11
Andoloner Katha (Mamata Banerjee), 95, 106
Angaria, Chhoto, 186, 187
Anubhuti (Mamata Banerjee), 51
Ashutosh College, 26
Association for Protection of Democratic Rights (APDR), 74, 177–78

Bahujan Samaj Party (BSP), 4, 5, 79, 81
Baidik, Pancham, 120
Bandyopadhyay, Ajitesh, 129
Bandyopadhyay, Debabrata, 197
Bandyopadhyay, Manik, 128
Bandyopadhyay, Sudip, 8, 29, 43–44, 52, 58, 166, 170
Bandyopadhyay, Tarashankar, 128
Banerjee, Gayetri (mother), 7, 8–9, 16, 61, 72, 165
Banerjee, Kalyan, 62
Banerjee, Mamata
    authoritarian streak/ highhandedness, 167–71
    birth, 7
    childhood, 8–9
    communication style/syntax, 6, 12–13, 15–16, 19, 21, 32, 77, 78, 80, 91, 130, 132, 146–47, 154

conflicted personality, 2–6,
35–36, 44, 66, 78, 117,
167, 176, 185, 198
Congress complex, 28–30,
32–42, 47;—broke away
from, 24–25, 40–41
defiant and aggressive woman,
3, 10, 93, 118, 131, 143
Gandhian way of living, 83
Hazra junction, attack, 7, 18,
61–65, 93
early years as an MP, 7
relationship with feminism,
71–72
friends and foes, 179–83
home and world, 7–11
ideology of humanism, 4, 21,
95, 131, 133
and Maoists, 105–12
and Mayawati, 5, 45, 73–74,
79, 80–84, 87–88
relationship with NDA, 37,
39, 42–55
outspokenness, 165
relationship with party,
165–74
in politics, 1–2, 12–14, 24–32
lower-middle-class
background, 3, 6, 11, 12,
76, 77, 94
painting exhibitions, 163–64
lack of personal life, 10
policy and administration,
194–95

as railway minister, 21, 22,
39, 45, 50, 82, 93, 145,
150–54, 155–59, 180,
195–96
religiosity, 16–19, 130
resurrection, 91–96
shrill negativism, 6
superstition and spirituality,
15–22
victim of vilification, 29
threat to hang herself, 6, 40
writings, 11, 20–21
Banerjee, Pankaj, 43
Banerjee, Pradip, 97–98, 105,
167–68
Banerjee, Promileswar (father),
7–8, 33, 72
Banerjee, Victor, 175
Bankura, 106
Bantala case, 70–71
Basu, Anil, 66, 186, 190
Basu, Bratya, 119, 121, 123–24,
136, 165, 184, 198
Basu, Hemanta, 186, 187
Basu, Jyoti, 48, 184, 191
Basu, Samaresh, 128
Belur Math, 17, 22, 132
Bengal Renaissance, 67
Bengali middle classes, 11, 14,
77, 78, 92
Bhadra, Sujato, 74, 105, 127, 137,
162, 165, 168, 170,198
bhadralok aesthetics, 77, 88, 94,
142

disintegration, 12–15, 138
dominance, 14
quintessential, 18–19
Bhagalpur riot criminals, 185
Bharat Sevasram Sangha, 134
Bharatchandra, 121
Bharatiya Janata Party (BJP), 4, 6, 41, 44–52, 54, 56, 87, 91, 99, 103, 113, 151, 164, 174
Bhatia, Sabeer, 139, 142
Bhattacharjee, Buddhadeb, 54, 102, 104, 106, 110, 120, 125–28, 143, 145, 159, 172–73, 179–80, 184, 190, 195
Bhattacharyya, Dwaipayan, 33–34
Bhattacharya, Nabarun, 15
Bhattacharya, Rabindranath, 96
Bhattacharya, Sukanta, 125, 129, 134, 153
Bhowanipur Girls' School, 9
Bhumi Uchchhed Pratirodh Committee, 102
Bhunia, Manas, 182
Birati case, 70–71
Biswas, Debabrata, 123
Biswas, Hemango, 123
Biswas, Moinak, 13–15, 132
Bose, Biman, 190
Bose, Krishna, 11, 30–31, 33, 42, 46, 50–51, 73, 85–86, 100, 127, 195
Bose, Purnendu, 105
Bose, Sisir, 30, 33

Bose, Subhash Chandra, 42
Brahmo tradition in Bengal, 121
Budhia, Sanjay, 195
Bureau of Industrial and Financial Reconstruction (BIFR), 53
Burn Standard Company, 158
bus fair hike, street protests in Kolkata, 23–24

caste norms, prejudices, 1, 2, 7, 20, 80–81, 199
Central Bureau of Investigation (CBI), 90–91, 114
Chakraborty, Sandipan, 195
Chatterjee, Anima, 2
Chatterjee, Asim, 97, 136–37
Chatterjee, Partha, 89
Chatterjee, Somnath, 27–29, 93
Chhatra Parishad (CP), 25, 27
Chidambaram, P., 111, 172, 173
Chowdhury, Salil, 100, 123, 133
Centre for Indian Trade Unions (CITU), 134
class struggle, class prejudices, 12, 19, 20, 69, 71, 77, 84–85, 90, 92, 94, 128–30, 147
Communist Party of India (Marxist) (CPI-M), 4, 7, 14, 45–50, 53–55, 62–65, 66–72, 78–79, 84–88
and Congress, alliance, 41–42
cultural lineage, 116–20, 122–23, 126, 129–30

discomfiture, 115
disconnected from masses, 5, 145
gender politics, 10
armed militias (Harmad Vahini), 108, 110–11, 170, 172
Mamata/Trinamool Congress entente, 3, 6, 10–11, 24, 26–28, 31–32, 34–35, 90, 118–19, 141, 142, 149–51, 156–57, 161–62, 167, 170–73, 176, 179–81, 184, 186–87, 189–94, 199
organizational structure, 59–60, 160–61, 180
partisan politics, 176
and Singur–Nandigram struggle, 11, 89–93, 94, 96, 98, 100, 102–04, 107–11, 121–22, 131, 134, 136–38, 143, 156
Students' Federation of India (SFI), 25, 194
Congress, Congress (I), 1–2, 4, 23, 24, 27, 33–34, 37–42, 46, 61, 63–64, 67, 73–74, 80, 82, 87, 121, 141, 147, 153, 162
anti-Congress wave, 35
CPI (M) entente, 40
defeated BJP led NDA, 54, 56–57
gender politics, 72
Mamata, relations, 42–44
perennial factional feuds, 25, 33, 44, 172
repressed Naxalites, 24
lack of strength, 28–29
resurgence, 31, 41
Singur–Nandigram issue, 98, 103–04, 106
and Trinamool Congress, relations, 4, 6, 50
Contractor, Nari, 74
crimes against women, 70
cultural spaces, transformation, 18, 66, 113–38, 200
Cummings, E.E., 126

Das Gupta, Gurudas, 48
Das, Brindaban, 65
Das, Malati, 65
Dasgupta, Swapan, 147, 148
Dasmunshi, Deepa, 172
Deb, Gautam, 184, 189
Democratic Socialist Organization (DSO), 25
Dev, Santosh Mohan, 86
Dey, Bishnu, 128
Dravida Munnetra Kazhagam (DMK), 36, 49
Durga Puja, 15, 195
Dutt, Utpal, 122, 123, 129
Dutta, Anjan, 15
Dutta, Sudhindranath, 129
Dwikhandita (Taslima Nasreen), 116

INDEX 211

Ekante (Mamata Banerjee, 2003), 9, 11, 15, 16, 75
Election Commission, 44, 136, 150, 180
elections, general
 1984, 27, 30, 31, 63
 1989, 23, 35, 39
 1991, 35
 1996, 40
 1998, 46, 47
 2004, 53–54, 56
 2009, 56, 97, 110, 122–23, 166, 169–70, 176
election, West Bengal assembly
 1977, 27
 1982, 30
 2006, 125, 159
 2011, 22, 30, 32–33, 57, 111, 120, 136, 144, 163
Emergency, 80
Engels, Friedrich, 134

Faulkner, William, 126
Federation of Indian Chambers of Commerce and Industries (FICCI), 174
feminism, 10, 68–72
Fernandes, George, 51
Fernandes, Oscar, 43
feudalism, 128
Ford, Richard, 125
Forward Bloc, 42, 98, 186–87

Gananatya Sangha, 123

Ganashakti (Suman Kabir), 108
Gandhi, Gopalkrishna, 100, 114, 125
Gandhi, Indira, 1, 26–28, 33, 34, 42, 80
Gandhi, M.K., 82, 83–84, 153, 164
Gandhi, Rahul, 34, 182
Gandhi, Rajiv, 1, 23–24, 30, 32–33, 34, 36, 43, 61, 64, 72–74, 182
Gandhi, Sonia, 34, 42–43, 73–74, 182–83
Gangopadhyay, Sunil, 122
gender and sexual politics, 10, 65–77, 81, 90
George, Vincent, 23
Ghatak, Ritwik, 122, 123, 129, 130
Ghosh, Arpita, 13, 72, 78, 119–21, 124, 165
Ghosh, Dipak, 184
Ghosh, Ranjit, 26
Ghosh, Tapan, 187
Ghosal, Prabir, 27, 31, 63
Ginsberg, Allen, 126, 130
Goenka, Sanjeev, 195
Goethe, 129
Goswami, Joy, 120
Groys, Boris, 140, 143
Guevara, Che, 109
Guha, Ramachandra, 147
Gujarat: post-Godhra pogrom (2002), 5, 45, 51, 99

Gujral, I.K., 36
Gupta, Dipankar, 147
Gupta, Manish, 184, 198
Gyaneshwari Express accident, 111, 151

Haldia Petrochemical project, 32
Halim, H.A., 186
Haug, Frigga, 71
Hindutva politics, 4, 52. *See also* Bharatiya Janata Party
Hudson, Rock, 74
human rights, 161, 178
humanism, humanitarianism, 4, 7, 21, 95, 131, 133

Indian National Trade Union Congress (INTUC), 27
Indian People's Theatre Association (IPTA), 14, 100, 124, 129, 131
Indo-US Nuclear Deal, 55
industrialization, 54, 69, 92, 100–01, 156–57, 174, 178, 188, 193

Jadavpur constituency, 23, 27–29, 35, 63, 118
Jago Bangla, 163
Jain Commission, 36–37
Jalan, M.K., 195
Janata Dal (Secular), 98
Janatar Darbars (people's courts), 177
Jangalmahal, 105, 106 168, 173
Jangipur constituency, 42
Jayalalithaa, J., 73–74
Joardar, Aboni, 184
Jogamaya Devi College, Kolkata, 25, 27
Josh, Swarnalata, 186
Joy, Sindhu, 72

Kali worship, 16–17
Kanshi Ram, 74, 79, 81–82. *See also* Mayawati
Kashi Mitra burning ghat, 21
Kesri, Sitaram, 44
Khondakar, Akbar, 86
Khurshid, Salman, 147, 148
Kishenji, 173–74
Kolar coach factory, 156
Kolkata Metro Railway extension project, 22
Kolkata Municipal Corporation (KMC), 21–22, 49, 54, 56, 135, 136, 181
Konar, Benoy, 67, 186

Lalgarh movement, 60, 89–112, 127, 167, 173, 187
Land Acquisition Bill (2011), 196–97
Land Commission for West Bengal, 197
land question, 195–97. *See also* Singur and Nandigram movements

Left Front, 5, 14, 19, 23, 24, 27, 29

Mahasweta Devi, 32, 72, 99, 107, 116, 178, 181
Mahato, Chhatradhar, 107
Mahato, Padma, 184
Mahato, Umakanta, 111
Majlis-e-Ittehadul Muslimeen (MIM), 115
Malik, Debu, 91
Malik, Monoranajan, 91
Malik, Surajit, 91
Malik, Tapasi, 70, 89–91, 98, 118, 120, 168
Mandal Commission Report, 79
Marx, Karl, 130, 134
Mayawati, 5, 45, 73–74, 79, 80–84, 87–88
    faced discrimination as a girl child, 81
    blatant display of wealth, 82
Mazdoor Kranti Parishad, 98
Meakan, G.S., 195
media, role, 13, 143, 147–48
Medinipur, 48, 105,
Mitra, Amit, 174, 183, 184, 198
Mitra, Ashok, 129
Mitra, Sambhu, 123, 129
Mitra, Saonli, 119
Mitra, Somen, 40, 41, 43, 44, 166
Modi, Narendra, 5, 51, 185
Mukherjee, Barnali, 97, 176
Mukherjee, Geeta, 48

Mukherjee, Jiban, 184
Mukherjee, Pranab, 41–42, 43, 126, 168, 182
Mukherjee, Subrata, 1–2, 26–28, 32–33, 40, 41, 49, 98, 104
Mukhopadhyay, Subhash, 123

Nandan, 125
Nandigram. *See* Singur and Nandigram movements
Nandy, Amitava, 180
Narayan, Jayaprakash, 5, 80
Narayanan, K.R., 50
Narmada Bachao Andolan (NBA), 74
Nasreen, Tasleema, 5
Nasreen, Taslima, 5, 115–17
National Advisory Council, 183
National Democratic Alliance (NDA), 4–5, 37, 39, 42–54, 113, 150, 166, 167
National Sports Welfare Fund, 163
Naxal movement, Naxalites, 24, 90
Nazrulgeeti, 145
Nehru, Jawaharlal, 74
Neotia, Harsh, 195
Nigam, Aditya, 83–84
Nishaaner Naam Tapasi Malik (Kabir Suman), 98, 118, 168
Nitish Kumar, 51, 53, 159–65, 171, 175, 179, 185

Obama, Barack, 105, 188
Operation Barga, 197
opportunism, 4, 87, 137

Pal, Tapas, 119, 166
Panja, Ajit, 44, 49–50, 52
Panskura constituency, 48–49, 166
Parichaya, 129
Party for Democratic Socialism (PDS), 98, 169–70
Paschim Banga Ganatantrik Mahila Samiti (PBGMS), 66, 70
Paschim Banga Khet Mazdoor Samiti (PBKMS), 98, 177–78
Paswan, Ram Vilas, 6, 86, 145
Patkar, Medha, 68, 74
People's Committee against Police Atrocities (PCPA), 106, 107
People's Democratic Conference of India (PDCI), 113
Poshu Khamar, 120
Pulishi Santrash Birodhi Janasadharaner Committee (People's Committee against Police Atrocities), 106
Purulia, 106
Putatunda, Samir, 98

Rabinbabu, 100
Rabindrasangeet, 3, 11, 30, 100, 123, 127, 128, 129, 133, 135–36, 144, 145
Rabitirtha, 135
Radhakrishnan, S., 195
Rajendra Prasad, 153
Rajinder Sachar Committee Report (2006), 114–15
Ram temple issue, 52
Ramachandran, M.G. (MGR), 74
Ramakrishna Paramahansa, 16, 18–22, 42, 121, 130–34
Ramaswamy, V., 121–22
Rao, Narasimha, 5, 35, 38, 75, 163
Rashtriya Janata Dal (RJD), 85, 160, 180
Ray, Raka, 66, 70
Ray, Satyajit, 66
Rehman, Rizwanur, 11, 114–17
Roy, Bani Sinha, 100
Roy, Jiten, 186
Roy, Mukul, 89, 100, 158
Roy, Prafulla Chandra, 153
Roy, Saugata, 16, 32, 41, 57, 62, 97
Roy, Shatabdi, 67, 119
Ruddhasangeet (The Song that Was Stifled), 123

Sachar, Rajinder, 114–15
Safwi, H.A., 184
Sain Bari murder case, 186–87
Sain, Moloy, 186
Sain, Pranab, 186
Salim Group of industries, 54, 102

Samajwadi Party, 85, 98
Sarada Devi, 21, 121, 132, 133
Sarkar, Abhirup, 100–02, 104, 149, 155, 157, 159, 160–61, 183, 198
Sarkar, Sumit, 18–19
secularism–communalism axis, 4, 45
Sen, Binayak, 188
Sen, Dola, 105
Sen, Mrinal, 122
Sen, Nirupam, 186–87
Sen, Prafulla, 164
Sengupta, Barun, 63
Seth, Lakshman, 103
Seth, Suhel, 147, 148
Singh, Manmohan, 55
Singur and Nandigram movements, 5, 11, 12, 20, 47, 55, 58–59, 67, 71, 78, 80, 89–112, 118, 121–22, 131, 156–57, 168, 170, 173, 176–77, 196
Singur Krishi Jami Raksha Committee (SKJRC), 96–97, 167
social consciousness, 175–76
Socialist Unity Centre of India (SUCI), 25, 90
South Kolkata constituency, 40
Sriram, Hariharan, 139
Struggle for Existence (Mamata Banerjee, 1998), 1, 11, 164, 177

Suman, Kabir, 37, 97, 98–99, 103, 108–09, 113, 117–19, 127, 168–69
Suvaprasanna, 119, 163

Tagore, Rabindranath, 37, 127, 128, 130–31, 136
Tarapith, 16
Tata Nano factory, land acquisition for, 89, 92, 99–100, 102, 157, 178, 195, 197
Tebhaga movement, 131, 132
Tehelka's defence deals expose, 49
Terrorist and Disruptive Activities (Prevention) Act (TADA), 5, 35, 36, 37, 38, 169
Thakur, Anukul, 153
Todi, Ashok, 114
Trinamool (2010), 11
Trinamool Congress, 2–4, 6, 8, 10–14, 16, 18, 20–21, 24, 29–30, 32–35, 37, 41, 56–57, 62, 64–67, 71–73, 78, 82, 86, 89–90, 92–97, 100, 103, 105–11, 113–15, 126–28, 130, 134–35, 137–39, 150, 152–53, 155–57, 161, 164–72, 175–77, 180–87, 191–92, 196–98
and Congress, electoral alliance, 40, 50
culture in, 117–24
relationship with Maoists, 173–74

and NDA, 42–55
organizational structure, 58–60
Tripathi, Kamlapati, 1–2
2G spectrum allocation, 163

United Front, 36, 40, 43
United Progressive Alliance (UPA), 32, 39, 52, 167, 169, 174, 196
Upadhyay, Barnali, 98
Upadhyay, Bijoy, 98
Uttam Kumar, 135, 153

Vajpayee, Atal Bihari, 5, 45–46, 49, 51, 150, 165
Viswa-Bharati University, 123
Vivekananda, 16, 18, 21, 22, 37, 106, 121, 131–33

West Bengal
economy and development, big push theory, 155–59
politics, 3, 14, 24, 40–41, 65, 66, 79, 90, 111
President's rule, 48–49
Pradesh Congress Committee (WBPCC), 36, 40, 182
Youth Congress, 33, 64, 172
Whitman, Walt, 126, 130
Women's Reservation Bill, 85–86

Yadav, Lalu Prasad, 45, 79, 80, 86, 140–42, 146, 150, 160, 171
Yadav, Mulayam Singh, 79, 80, 86

Acknowledgements

This book would not have been possible without my family: Anirban Gupta Nigam, Aditya Nigam, Nivedita Menon, Bishnupriya Gupta, V. Bhaskar and Dhruva Bhaskar. Their invaluable support was important at every stage. Basabi Sarbadhikari and Atasi Roy's warm hospitality in Kolkata; Deepayan Chatterjee's reading the manuscript at short notice and offering comments; and Diptosh Majumdar's insights were all crucial to the researching, writing and editing process. In Kolkata, Prabir Ghosal's generous sharing of information and experiences was invaluable. Access to Dilip Banerjee's amazing collection of photographs, and careful copy-editing by Sunrita Sen and Ajitha G.S. helped see the book through. I would like to thank Shantanu Ray Chaudhuri for his efforts on behalf of the book. Sheema Mookherjee first put the book into motion, for which I thank her.